RED, GREEN & BEYOND

BY NANCY HORNBACK

AND TERRY CLOTHIER THOMPSON

Red, Green and Beyond
By Nancy Hornback and Terry Clothier Thompson

Edited by Judy Pearlstein
Technical edit by Shannon Richards
Design by Amy Robertson
Photographs by Aaron Leimkuhler
Illustrations by Lon Eric Craven
Quilting illustrations by Gail Hand
Production Assistance by Jo Ann Groves

Published by Kansas City Star Books
1729 Grand Boulevard
Kansas City, Missouri 64108

First edition, first printing
ISBN: 978-1-933466-54-5

Printed in the United States of America
By Walsworth Publishing Co.
Marceline, Missouri

To order copies, call StarInfo, 816-234-4636 (say "Operator")

PickleDish.com
The Quilter's Home Page

Dedicated to past, present, and future appliqué artists.

Background: Nancy McKelvey McGill,
of Tennessee, quilted her hand print
near the center of the *Rose of Sharon*
quilt with her name embroidered in
white. N.M.Mc. Oct. 30, 1889, Age 73.

Contents

Acknowledgments

Publisher: Doug Weaver
Editor: Judy Pearlstein
Book designer: Amy Robertson
Photography: Aaron Leimkuehler, Tom Pott
Illustrator: Lon Eric Craven
Technical editor: Shannon Richards
Production assistant: Jo Ann Groves

A special thank you to Gail Hand for drafting quilting patterns

Lenders of 19th and 20th Century Quilts:
* Bari Garst
* Mary Louise Newcomb Heaton
* Dorothy Kimbell
* Adelia Hanson
* Donald W. Holtgraver, Sr. and Ann Holtgraver
* Iowa State Historical Society
* Wichita-Sedgwick County Historical Society
* Elizabeth Pett

21st Century Quiltmakers:
* Joan Bruce
* Debra Reimer Burgess
* Barbara Collins
* Gail L. Hand
* Cheryl Harp
* Barb Fife
* Rene Jennings
* Susan Martin
* Ilyse Moore
* Barbara Nickelson
* Andi Perejda
* Mindy Peterson
* Marlene Royse
* RoRi Matters Stoller

Professional Machine Quilters:
* Debra Freese
* Kim Hull
* Lori Kukuk

Research Assistance:
* Jodene Evans, Iowa Historical Society
* Jamie Frazier Tracy, Wichita-Sedgwick County Historical Society
* Mary Madden, Rebecca J. Martin, Joy Brennan, Kansas State Historical Society
* Loretta Stuber, Greenwood County, KS Historical Society
* Lora Topinka, Sumner County, KS Historical Society
* Indiana State Library
* Bari Garst
* Adelia and Bert Hanson
* Mary Louise Newcomb Heaton
* Wanda Lawrence Hildyard
* Donald J. Holtgraver. Jr.
* Dorothy Kimbell
* Harley Lawrence
* Martha Jo Longhofer
* Susan Price Miller
* Elizabeth Pett
* Bets Ramsey
* Merikay Waldvogel

Others Who Helped:
* Merilyn Austin
* Marilyn Coberly
* Cheryl Harp
* Ann Harrod
* Ellen Horn
* Jack Webb
* Mary N. Williams

Introduction

Nancy Hornback and Terry Thompson have collected red and green 19th Century quilts, and stories of the makers, for over 30 years. When we wrote our first collaborative book *Quilts in Red and Green-and the Women Who Made Them*, in 2006, we had hard decisions to make about which quilts to include in the book. Thanks to Doug Weaver, our Kansas City Star publisher, who agreed to a second red and green book.

We wanted to combine the traditional early 19th Century designs with 21st Century quilt makers using modern and diverse fabrics and sewing methods for today's quilt makers.

With phone calls and letters, Terry and Nancy recruited friends from coast to coast—one in North Carolina, a group of four in California, and seven Kansas quilters.

We began our search with a meeting over lunch in a local bookstore in Wichita, Kansas. We showed pictures of the older quilts and asked our quilters to choose a quilt that interested them and could be finished by the deadline for editing, photography, graphic design and proofreading. Using the old applique' designs, they created their own versions. We encourage you to use the templates to create your own version.

The women whose 21st Century quilts appear in this book took this project very seriously, met all the deadline dates, and let us borrow their quilts for months so that we could plan and write the book. Their sense of color,

design, and perfect workmanship created eleven phenomenal quilts (yes, we included Terry's and Nancy's quilts too) way beyond our expectations.

While they stitched, Nancy discovered some wonderful stories and details about the original 19th Century artists. Terry spent her time writing directions for the vintage quilts, mostly from pictures, and some from the actual quilt.

Our new quilt makers expressed great joy in the process of creating a new interpretation of a 19th Century quilt, using the traditional pattern as a starting point. We could not contain our surprise and pleasure at such innovation and creativity these piecers and appliqué artists expressed using the traditional appliqué patterns.

It is our great joy to present our second book on 19th Century appliqué quilts and the women who made them, this time including our 21st Century quilt artists.

— *Nancy and Terry*

Blooming Buds and Berries
84" x 84"
Unknown Maker
Collection of Nancy Hornback

Unknown Maker
Blooming Buds and Berries

This quilt was bought in an antique shop and it was not possible to learn the name of the maker or where the quilt was made. It is often the case that the identities of nineteenth century quilt makers have been separated from their quilts. This lost history makes us sad and reinforces the encouragement for today's quilt makers to sign their quilts. At the least, we should put a label on the back of the quilt with a signature, place and date, using a good indelible ink that is friendly to fabric. For further suggestions on how to label and document your quilt, see *Quilters' Stories: Collecting History in the Heart of America* by Deb Rowden (Kansas City Star Books, 2005).

In this variation of a vase and flowers pattern, five large appliquéd motifs are set alternately with plain white blocks. The symme-try of the three-stemmed blossom design has been slightly varied by the irregular placement of leaves. The primary floral motif is a 12-lobed rosette appliquéd in layers of red, orange, and white. Small rosette flowers are on side stems. In the center of each of the four borders is a vase of flowers. In vases on two opposing sides of the quilt are arrangements of red buds and blossoms. In the other two borders, ferns enclose a flower-like decoration composed of six padded circles on a red stem. The vines sprouting from the vases spread across the borders, connecting with each other and supporting stems of green, red, yellow, and white berries. The quilt contains over 675 padded berries. Quilting is closely worked in parallel lines. The plain white blocks between the appliquéd motifs are quilted in double feather wreaths.

Starburst Buds and Berries
85" X 89"
Hand appliquéd by Barbara J. Nickelson, Wichita, Kansas
Machine quilted by Debra Freese, Wichita, Kansas

Unknown Maker
Blooming Buds and Berries

84" x 84" • Instructions for quilt on page 2

Estimated Yardage
* 7 1/2 yds white or ecru for blocks and borders
* 2 1/2 yds red
* 3 yds green
* 1 1/2 yds cheddar/gold

Cutting Direction for Pattern Pieces
* A – Cut 15 center circles, ecru or white.
* B – Cut 15 rosettes, red.
* C – Cut 15 rosettes, orange, yellow or gold.
* D – Cut 15 rosettes, red.
* E – Cut 20 center circles, orange, yellow, gold.
* F – Cut 20 rosettes (small), ecru or white.
* G – Cut 20 rosettes (small), red.
* H – Cut 5 large buds, red.
* I – Cut 5 large calyx, green.
* J – Cut 10 small calyx, green.
* K – Cut 10 small buds, red.
* L– Cut 40 leaves, green.
* Cut 5 background squares 20 1/2".
* Cut 4 – 20 1/2" squares for plain blocks.

For Borders
For vase #1
* CC – Vase #1, cut 2 green.
* N – Leaf and stem, cut 2 green.
* R – Cut 2 red.
* S – Buds, cut 4 red.
* X – Buds, cut 4, red.
* Y – Calyx, cut 2, green.

For vase #2
* P – Border sprigs, cut 2, reverse 2, green.
* T – Vase #2, cut 2, green.
* U – For handles, cut 2, reverse 2, green.
* UV — Leaf, cut 2, reverse 2, green.
* V – Berries, cut 36 red for vase #2.
* W – Calyx, cut 2, reverse 2, green.
* M – Buds, cut 4, red.
* XZ – Berries, cut 6 green, 2 red, and 4 orange.
* TT – Stems, cut 2 red.

Border Vines
* O – Border leaves, cut 29 green.
* ST – Stem, cut 29, green.

Continued on page 6.

Continued from page 5.

* Q – Circles, cut 192 green, 96 oranges, 120 light green, and 156 red.
* FF – Stems, with berries hanging from the main vine — cut 46-49 or embroider in red and green chain stitches 46 to 49 stems. There are 10 to 12 berries on each stem with red, orange and green berries; 9 stems show berries that are white and are barely visible on the vintage quilt. Instead of white berries (depending on the color of your background), substitute yellow, orange or gold berries.

Sewing Instructions

* Prepare all appliqués for hand or machine appliqué
* Notice that this block lies on its side with the bud in one corner. This allows more room for the large rosettes to bloom. For 1/2" finished bias stems, cut 1" long bias strips for stems and border vines.
* Follow instructions for turning under seam allowance with a 1" Clover bias maker in General Directions.
* Pin, baste and sew one rosette C over D, B over C – and circle A last. Make 3 large rosettes.
* Repeat process for the 4 small rosettes E, F, G
* Place 1/2" x 25" bias strip for center stem and 4 strips 9" long for right and left rosettes and 2 small rosettes. Cut a 6" strip for the bottom 2 rosettes.
* Place bud calyx I in corner, with bud H, then lay out stems, and appliqué large and small rosette units, following picture as a guide.
* Pin, baste and appliqué all units.

Border Directions

One of the interesting things Nancy and I discovered about this quilt is that there are 2 different designs in the middle of each opposite border. The vases are different as are the motifs sprouting from them. Both are unique. These details reveal the creative nature of the quiltmaker.

* Refer to General Directions starting on page 64 for 1/2" bias strips.
* Cut 2 borders for the top and bottom of finished quilt blocks — 12 1/2" x 60 1/2".
* Cut the 2 side borders 12 1/2" x 84 1/2".
* For the bias border vine, cut several 1" bias strips, enough to set into deep curves.
* Place vase #1 on bottom border and on the top border, referring to picture for placement, note that leaf U has a slit on the left leaf and none on the right ones.
* Pin, baste and appliqué vases, berries and leaves on each individual border, leaving long tails of the vines to be appliquéd in corners when all borders are sewn to body of quilt.

Setting Blocks and Borders

* See diagram on page 73.

Quilt and Bind

* Fill plain background blocks with lovely quilting designs. See pages 110-122. This quilt has a triple feathered wreath pattern with straight diagonal lines 1/2" apart, over the background.

Templates on pages 69-73.

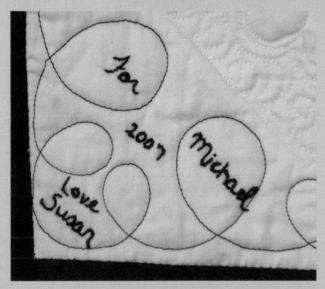

Shadows of the Past

Marlene Tamm Royse
Raleigh, Wake County, North Carolina
2007

Appliqué block from Cherry Basket quilt by
Mary Parks Lawrence, 1870

Made for a book by Terry Clothier Thompson
and Nancy Hornback
Original layout designed by Marlene Tamm Royse
12732 Little Creek Dr. Raleigh, NC 27603
919-661-8330

We encourage you to put a label on the back of your quilt with a signature, place and date, using a good indelible ink that is friendly to fabric.

Quilted by
Lori Kukuk

Rose of Sharon
84" x 90"
Sarah Ellen Knowles Fisher (1832-1925)
Made in Indiana in 1851.
Collection of Dorothy Kimbell

Sarah Fisher's
Rose of Sharon

A note handed down with this *Rose of Sharon* quilt states: "Made by Sarah Ellen (Knowles) Fisher about 1851. She was 19 years old. Born in 1832. Quilted by Unknown." According to the family, Sarah made it as a bride's quilt, although she did not marry for another fourteen years. Sarah was born in Gibson County, Indiana, daughter of Asa and Matilda Montgomery Knowles. She married Thomas S. Fisher in 1865 and with their small son Albert, they moved to Kansas before 1875, settling in the small town of Virgil. Thomas had injuries from the Civil War, and Sarah, known as "Aunt Sally" to family and friends, opened a hotel in her home to support the family. A second son, Joseph, was born in 1875. Sarah left the *Rose of Sharon* quilt to Joseph, who passed it on to two daughters and a son. One of those daughters, Dorothy Kimbell, now in her 90s, has fond memories of her grandmother. "We thought a lot of Grandma. She was a wonderful person." An oil boom in the region in 1915 brought new population to Virgil. Dorothy's parents were busy with a grocery store and a café, and so Dorothy and her siblings spent a lot of time with their grandmother. "She wore long skirts. If we asked her for money, she would lift her skirt and reach into a pocket in her petticoat to get nickels and dimes for us."

Sarah Fisher died in 1925 at the age of 92.

The appliqué pattern of Sarah Fisher's quilt consists of four sprouting flower stems extending from the layered center to the corners of the block, interspersed with stems of pomegranates. The strict symmetry of the design is broken by the addition of a tiny single bud at the base of each of the eight radiating stems, creating a feeling of motion. Undulating vines spiked with blossoms and buds echoing the flowers of the blocks are displayed on wide appliquéd borders on two sides of the quilt. The background is quilted in feather wreaths and double lines of cross-hatching. Quilted flowers on stems are linked to the appliquéd stems.

Sarah Ellen Knowles Fisher, age about 65. Courtesy of Dorothy Kimbell.

Below: Ladies' Aid Society, 1918, Virgil, Kansas. Sarah Fisher is third from the right in the first row. Courtesy of Greenwood County Historical Society
Lower left: Dorothy Kimbell, granddaughter of Sarah Fisher, Yates Center, Kansas, 2007. Photo by Ann Harrod.

Midnight Garden Memories
68" x 69"
Hand appliquéd by Mindy Peterson, Spring Hill, Kansas
Machine quilted by Lori Kukuk, McLouth, Kansas

Sarah Fisher's
Rose of Sharon

84" x 90" • Instructions for quilt on page 8

Estimated Yardage
* 7 1/4 yds white for blocks and borders
* 2 1/2 to 3 yds red
* 3 yds green
* 1 1/2 yds yellow, or cheddar gold

Cutting
* Cut 6 — 24 1/2" squares.
* A — Cut 6 circles, yellow.
* B — Cut 6 rosettes, red.
* C — Cut 42 large buds, red.
* D — Cut 42 calyx of large buds, yellow/gold.
* E — Cut 24 small buds, red.
* F — Cut 132 leaves on stems, green.
* G — Cut 24 pineapples, red.
* H — Cut 24 pineapple calyx, green.
* I — Cut 48 green bud calyx for blocks. For borders, cut 18 and 18 reverse.
* J — Cut 84 buds, red.
* K — Cut 48 medium leaves for small bud, green.
* L — Cut 72 small leaves for pineapple, green.
* M — Cut 72 leaves for border, green.
* N — Cut 24 large leaves, reverse 24 for blocks, red.
* Cut 48 large leaves, reverse 48 for blocks, green.
* Cut 36 large leaves, reverse 36 for borders, red,
* Cut 54 large leaves, reverse 54 for borders, green.
* O — Cut 18 buds, red.
* P — Cut 18 bud bottoms, yellow.
* Q — Cut 18 bud calyx, green.
* R — Cut 6 rosettes, yellow.

Sewing Directions
* Follow the color and number of pieces located on each pattern piece. Prepare appliqués for hand or machine appliqué.
* Cut 2 stems 1" x 17" for the pineapples, and 2 diagonal stems 1" x 24" for the buds. Cut off any excess after placing the buds and pineapples. Prepare stems with a 1" Clover bias maker.
* Lay out all pieces by beginning with the stems, short ones for the 2 pineapple 'G' units, and the 2 diagonal stems for the large bud 'D' units.
* Place rosette unit in center over stems in middle.
* Referring to the picture, place all prepared units, leaves, and buds on the blocks' pressed lines. Pin and baste in place.
* Appliqué all pattern pieces.

Borders
* Refer to diagram on page 76. Cut top and bottom borders 9 1/2" x 48 1/2" and cut 2 side borders 18 1/2" x 90 1/2".
* Appliqué borders referring to photo.
* Refer to diagram to set blocks and borders.

Quilt and Bind
* Quilting Designs — From the original quilt, choose a feathered circle wreath between the large bud and pineapple. Outline the quilt around the inside of each appliqué. Some have several rows 1/4" apart.

Templates on pages 74-76.

Cherry Baskets
72" x 84"
Made by Mary Parks Lawrence (1854-1950)
Kentucky, 1870
Collection of the Wichita-Sedgwick County Historical
Museum; gift of Marjorie Caskey and Douglas Caskey

Mary Parks' baby shoes, 1854, with
a gold leaf design of a vase and
flowers etched on the toe of each
shoe. It is interesting to think that
while the rest of the world saw the
design upside down, only baby Mary
saw it right side up.

Mary Parks Lawrence's
Cherry Baskets

A granddaughter of the woman who made this quilt describes her as "a gentle woman of petite stature." Born Mary Melvina Parks in 1854 in Logan County, Kentucky, she was the daughter of Leander S. Parks and Emily Luisa Henderson, and a fifth-generation descendant of a Scots-Irish immigrant to Pennsylvania. Growing up on her family's tobacco plantation, Mary became skilled in spinning, weaving, and quilting. She sewed garments for her father and four brothers, and her father told her he would buy a sewing machine if she would make coats for the family. When the sewing machine, bought from a traveling salesman, arrived in their home it was, her granddaughter told us, "a great day." In 1870, when she was sixteen years old, Mary traded some of her hand-woven goods for commercially manufactured fabrics to make her *Cherry Baskets* quilt. She hand pieced the red, pink, and orange parts of her floral motifs, but used her new sewing machine to appliqué the green stems and leaves. She also used the machine to quilt narrow white borders, although the body of the quilt was hand quilted.

Nineteenth century censuses show that Mary's maternal aunt, Margaret Henderson, lived with the Parks family for many years. Her occupation was listed as "seamstress." It is not difficult to imagine that Mary learned her needle skills from her aunt as well as her mother.

Mary came to Kansas by train with her parents in 1878 to homestead in Sumner County, near the Oklahoma border. In 1881 she married William

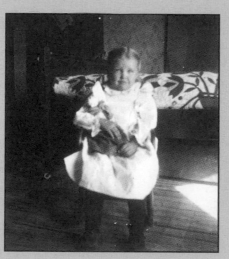

Mary Lawrence's daughter Eunice, c. 1906, with the Cherry Baskets quilt on a bed in the background.

Lawrence, a cattleman and widower from an adjoining farm. In addition to her husband's five children, Mary was a loving mother to six children of her own, two of whom died in early childhood. Flowers are again significant in Mary's life as seen in the two gravestones of these babies. Carved on each marker is a sprig of flowers with one broken blossom — a poignant symbol of the vulnerability of young children's lives in those times. Mary Parks Lawrence died in 1950 at the age of 96 and is buried between her husband and two young daughters.

The *Cherry Baskets* quilt displays a classic vase and flowers design. The two-handled urn holds a center stem with a large tulip in full bloom. Side stems with partial blooms are symmetrically arranged on both sides of the center stem. Overhanging the vase on either side are stalks bearing clusters of padded cherries. Background areas behind the motifs are hand quilted in one-fourth inch diagonal lines. Open spaces are hand quilted with feather wreaths and running feather designs.

The unusual arrangement of the blocks — nine full urns and three half urns — might be explained by a photograph that shows the *Cherry Baskets* quilt on a bed. Evidently the quilt was intended to be used on a bed that was against a wall.

Shadows of the Past
58" × 58"
Machine appliquéd and quilted by Marlene Tamm Royse,
Raleigh, North Carolina

Mary Parks Lawrence's
Cherry Baskets

72" x 77" • Instructions for quilt on page 12

Estimated Yardage
* 6 1/2 yds white
* 1 1/2 yds pink
* 2 yds red
* 2 1/2 yds green
* 1/2 yd orange

Cutting Directions for Pattern Pieces
* A – Top of vase — Cut 12 cheddar or gold .
* B – Cut 12 red.
* C – Cut 12 pink.
* D – Cut 12 red.
* E – Cut 12 pink.
* F – Cut 12 red.
* G – Cut 12 cheddar.
* H – Cut 12 center stem, teal blue.
* I – Cut 12, reverse 12 for left and right middle stems, teal blue.
* J – Cut 12, reverse 12 for left and right small lower stems, teal blue.
* K – Cut 120 leaves, teal.
* L – Cut 48 centers of flowers, cheddar — flowers are pieced.
* M – Cut 48 , reverse 48, pink.
* N – Cut 48, reverse 48 red .
* O – Cut 48, reverse 48, teal.
* P – Cut 12, reverse 12 for large flower, teal.
* Q – Cut 12, reverse 12 for large flower, red.
* R – Cut 12, reverse 12 for large flower, pink.
* S – Cut 12, reverse 12 for large flower, red.
* T – Cut 12 for large flower, cheddar.
* U – Cut 192 cherries, red.
* V – Cut 12, reverse 12 for stems for cherries, teal.
* W – Cut 12, reverse 12 for basket handles, teal.

We think Mary Parks Lawrence designed her Cherry Baskets quilt to fit the bed pictured with her daughter Eunice. This explains why she sewed 3 half blocks instead of 12 blocks. If you choose to make the 3 half blocks, follow the directions below.

* Cut 11 – 1/2" x 22 1/2" rectangles and 9 – 22 1/2" squares of white. Using the templates for the flower stems and basket, on the right side, cut out the shapes for just 1/2 of the block. Be sure to add a 1/4" seam allowance to all pieces that are on the edge of the cut block, which will be covered by the 3" border.

Sewing Directions for 12 Blocks
* Piece the two sides of the flower strips together in sections (see template). Add the bud, then join the two sides together.
* Piece the basket strips together. Add the basket top and handles.
* Arrange all pieces on the background block, following the pattern for placement. Pin or baste all in place.
* Appliqué.
* Embroider the cherry stems using an outline or chain stitch.

Continued on page 16.

Continued from page 15.

BORDERS
FOR 12 BLOCK QUILT:
* Cut top and bottom borders 3 1/2" x 88 1/2".
* Cut 2 side borders 3 1/2" x 72 1/2".

BORDERS FOR 9 FULL AND 3 HALF-BLOCKS:
* Cut top and bottom borders 3 1/2" x 77 1/2".
* Cut 2 side borders 3 1/2" x 72 1/2".
* Set blocks and borders referring to figure #1, page 79.

QUILT AND BIND
   Mary outlined each pattern piece seam, plus 1 quilted line down the center of each petal, stems and vase. See diagram on page 79 for quilting.
* To fill in areas behind the flowers, stems and leaves she quilted diagonal, parallel lines a scant 1/2" apart.
* Feathers descend from either side of vase.
* Feathered wreaths fill the space where the corners of the blocks meet. See Quilting Designs.
* Fill space between cherries with a small diamond of quilting.

Thanks to Deb Rowden for these Cherry Basket instructions. Deb featured Nancy Hornback and Terry Thompson in her wonderful book, Quilters Stories — Collecting History in the Heart of America. *Published by Kansas City Star Books. Look for it in your quilt stores, or PickleDish.com.*

TEMPLATES ON PAGES 77-79.

Above: Baby sunbonnet
Right: Child's turkey red calico dress with calico buttons (inset).

Coxcombs (above)
73" x 90"
Mary Ann Turley Morgan (1854-1917)
Indiana, 1869. Hand quilted by Edith Hornberger
Collection of Elizabeth Pett

Coxcombs (right)
Alice Rose Smith Klein
72" x 81"
Indiana, c. 1870
State Historical Society of Iowa, Des Moines

MARY ANN TURLEY'S
COXCOMBS

Mary Ann Turley Morgan; Courtesy of Elizabeth Pett

How wonderful it would be if all the quilts handed down from the 19th Century were so clearly marked to identify their makers as was this *Coxcomb* quilt. The quiltmaker appliquéd her name, "Mary A. Turley," and the date, "1869," in the lower right hand corner of the quilt's border.

Mary Ann Turley was born in Indiana in 1854, so we can determine that she was fifteen years old when she appliquéd her quilt top. Her parents were Mary Ann Guion and Thomas George Washington Turley. Mary Ann was the eighth child in their family of twelve children. The Turleys lived in Indianapolis until they moved to Kansas about 1870.

In 1871 Mary Ann married Levi Morgan in Fort Scott, Kansas. In 1885, Levi and Mary Ann took their family of six children by covered wagon to Morton County in the southwestern corner of Kansas, bordering Colorado and Oklahoma. Their daughter Catherine recalled their arrival: "We landed on as bare a prairie claim as can be imagined." The Morgans filed on a pre-emption claim and built a 12 foot by 20 foot soddy. They dug and cut the sods for the walls and used wood planks for the roof, covering it with sod and dirt. "Many nights when it rained Mother would put us all on the bed and put the wagon sheet over us to keep us dry." The family later built a dugout with two rooms, wooden sides, and a shingle roof. On Easter Sunday in 1887, a tornado struck the Morgan farm, blowing everything away. The family survived with only the clothes on their backs. Catherine wrote, "We were unable to save any belongings," but did not explain how her mother's *Coxcomb* quilt made it through the tornado. Mary Ann Turley's granddaughter Elizabeth Pett commented: "I have asked that same question my whole life!"

The eight blocks in Mary Ann's quilt are set on point, each with a cluster of large red and pink blossoms that

resemble coxcombs, with a single tulip-like bud at the top. Each group of flowers is placed in a feathery red and green half wreath. Between the large block designs are six smaller half wreaths, each with a single stem and two flowers, one a coxcomb and the other a tulip. In each of the four corners is a red and pink flower with five leaves in a sun wheel arrangement. Mary Ann used one side of her half wreaths for her border design.

When we saw this quilt, we had not ever seen another like it, so we were interested later to learn of one quite similar, made by a girl close to Mary Ann's age who also grew up in Indianapolis.* See page 18.

Alice used basically the same pattern as Mary Ann's, with some variations. There are nine blocks, set straight and side by side. Again, there are both coxcombs and tulips. Trailing vines with stems of tulips are in the top and bottom borders; the two side borders are left empty. Alice's blocks were appliquéd with a tiny herringbone stitch, a technique that suggests that these might have been blocks from an earlier time. Mary Ann's quilt top was not quilted until 1988. The edges of Alice's quilt top were hemmed, so it might be considered a counterpane or a summer spread.

These two look-alike quilts seem more than mere coincidence. Surely the two girls knew each other. Censuses and maps show they lived a few miles from each other in Indianapolis. Perhaps there was a yet undiscovered family connection; or maybe they attended the same church. At any rate, it seems certain that one girl shared her Coxcomb pattern with the other.

We have learned of another quilt, documented by the Tennessee Quilt Project, that is essentially this same pattern, with yet a third way of setting the blocks together.

Red and Green Jubilee
73" x 73"
Machine appliquéd and quilted by Cheryl Harp, Wichita, Kansas

Mary Ann Turley's
Coxcombs

80 1/2" x 96 3/4" • Instructions for quilt on page 18

Estimated Yardage

* 7 1/4 yds white or ecru for 8 — 20" squares, side setting triangles and corners.
* 3 yds red
* 3 yds green
* 2 1/2 yds pink

Cutting for Blocks and Borders

* Cut 8 — 20 1/2" squares.
* A — Cut 8, reverse 8, red inside leaf for 8 blocks.
* Cut 11, reverse 11, red, inside leaf for borders.
* B — Cut 8, reverse 8 green outside leaf for blocks.
* Cut 11, reverse 11 green for outside leaf for borders.
* C — Cut 48 pink flowers for blocks.
* Cut 32 red for flowers for blocks.
* Cut 6 red for flowers for borders for a combined total of 38 red.
* Cut 18 pink for borders—combined total of 66 pink.
* D — Cut 14 green calyx under all flower groups.
* E — Cut 6, reverse 6, red small inside split leaves for side triangles.
* Outside split leaf for side triangles, cut 6, reverse 6 green.
* F — Cut 14 red rose buds for blocks and setting triangles.
* G — Cut 14 green stems adding 18" to stem for 8 blocks.
* H — Cut 4 green circles for sunwheels in corners.
* I — Cut 4 red rosettes for sunwheels.
* J — Cut 4 pink rosettes for sunwheels.
* K — Cut 20 green leaves for sunwheels.
* L — Cut 14 red circles for ends of all stems.
* See diagram on page 84 for cutting, setting triangles and corners.

Templates on pages 80-84.

Sewing Directions
Blocks are set on point

* Begin with the large split-leaf leaves. Sew the inside red leaf to the large green leaf-reversing 1 leaf, for all 9 squares.
* Repeat for the smaller leaves in the side setting triangles.
* Appliqué rose bud F to G calyx (be sure to add 18" to the calyx stem for the 8 blocks.)
* Stack flowers C, beginning with the center row of four, red, pink, red, and pink. Appliqué as shown in quilt. Stack the right and left groups of 3 roses slightly turning them into a curve, as seen on quilt.
* Place calyx D under the center red rose and over the long center stems.
* Sew red circle L to the end of long stem.
* For the six side setting squares, repeat directions for the curved shorter split leaf E. There is only one rose unit, C — red in the center with 3 pink roses surrounding the red rose. Add the short calyx D underneath the red rose, and the L circle under the calyx.
* Place the red rose bud and calyx at the top of the top pink rose and sew in place. Repeat for 6 side triangles.
* Appliqué the 4 corners with the sunwheels. Layer green circle H, red rosette I and pink rosette J. Place the 5 leaves K referring to the drawing.
* Set the blocks — see diagram.

Borders

* Cut 1 border for the bottom of quilt, 12 1/2" x 57".
* Cut 2 side borders 12 1/2" x 97 1/4".
* Appliqué the large leaves onto the borders.
* Sew borders to quilt. See fig. #3 on page 84.

Quilt and Bind

Happy Berries
49" x 49"
Replica of quilt attributed to Sarah Stanley Tash, Indiana
Hand appliquéd by Nancy Hornback, sewing by Merilyn Austin and Ellen Horn, Wichita, Kansas.
Machine quilted by Debra Freese, Wichita, Kansas

SARAH STANLEY TASH'S
BERRIES

During a visit to her home in Stillwater, Oklahoma, Adelia Hanson showed us her family quilts. One in particular caught our attention. We liked its "folky" look, and Terry observed that berries on an appliquéd quilt give it a cheerful, happy look. We also liked the large center flower of bright turkey red and chrome orange and the clusters of pomegranates. See pomegranate detail below.

Unfortunately, over the years the quilt had become quite stained, too much so to be photographed for this book. We wanted to preserve the pattern, so we decided one of us would make a replica of the original quilt, and the other would make a contemporary version.

Adelia says she has only family legend to go by. Her maternal grandmother Nell Baker said that Grandmother Tash made the 'berries' quilt. Grandmother Tash actually would have been Nell's great-great grandmother, who died at age 89, four years before Nell was born. She surely heard the family talk about Grandmother Sarah Tash. Sarah Stanley was born in North Carolina in 1788, married John Tash in 1809, and moved with him in 1816 to Washington County Indiana, an area only beginning to be settled. Sarah lived on the Indiana Homestead for sixty years, and died in 1875. The quilt passed from mother to daughter through five generations.

On Sarah's quilt, a wide center stem with a large red and orange flower dominates the block. There are two side stems, each holding three pomegranates. Red and orange berries are scattered around the background, floating free, not attached to the stems.

Sarah Stanley Tash

Sarah Tash was featured in an article in *The Banner,* the newspaper in Pekin, Indiana, January 29, 1931:

Grandma Tash knew many things that people that live here now do not know — she knew how to spin tow, flax, and wool into threads, how to double and twist the threads and reel them into cuts, skeins, and hanks ready for the loom, and she knew exactly what to use to make a certain number of yards of jeans, flannel or lensey [sic] or what ever she needed.

She knew how to thread up the loom and weave the cloth and how to cut the cloth and make garments and bed clothing for a family of ten.

And besides all this, she knew how to live a life we never have heard criticized [sic].

Pomegranate detail from Berries

Terry's Berries
50" × 50"
Designed by Terry Clothier Thompson, machine appliquéd by Jean Stanclift, Lawrence, Kansas
Machine quilted by Lori Kukuk, McLouth, Kansas

Nancy's and Terry's
Berries

78" x 78" • Instructions for quilt on page 22

We both loved the folk art style of this quilt, and we each wanted to make our own interpretation of the design.

Nancy made a four block quilt using the traditional design and colors of the original quilt. Terry chose a really different background for her 36" block, a woven fabric that looks like a 19th Century woven coverlet. Terry also borrowed some patterns from the *Rose of Sharon* quilt, mixed and moved the designs to create a different look based on the vintage quilt.

The templates are marked for use in either quilt.

Nancy's Quilt
49" x 49"

Estimated Yardage
* 3 yds white for background squares and borders, based on 42" wide fabric.
* 1/4 yd red for 1 1/2" inside border.
* 1/2 yd gold for appliqué and berries.
* 2 yds green for appliquéd stems, leaves and pomegranates.
* 1/2 yd for rosettes, crowns, and berries, red.

Cutting Directions for Blocks and Borders:
* Cut 4 — 20 1/2" white squares for blocks.
* Cut 2 — 1" x 40 1/2" red top and bottom, 1/2" borders.
* Cut 2 — 1" x 41 1/2" red side 1/2" borders.
* Cut 2 — 5 1/2" x 41 1/2" white top and bottom borders.
* Cut 2 — 5 1/2" x 51 1/2" white side borders.

For Appliqués
* A — Cut 4, reverse 4, green for right and left stem. (Be sure to tape short stem A to top of long stem A.)
* B — Cut 17 red crowns.

* C — Cut 24 green pomegranates.
* D — Cut 24 gold rectangles 2" x 3" to fit under teardrop shape for reverse appliqué.
* d — Cut 24 red rectangles 2 1/2" x 1 1/2" for reverse appliqué.
* E — Cut 16 green leaves.
* F — Cut 32 red and 45 gold berries.
* H — Cut 5 gold rosettes.
* I — Cut 5 red circles, for rosette centers.
* J — Cut 1 green leaf #1.
* K — Cut 4 green leaves #2.
* L — Cut 7 green leaves #3.
* M — Cut 4 red rosettes for 4 corners.
* N — Cut 1 red for center rosette.
* Cut 4 center stems 1 1/2" X 18 1/2".

Sewing Directions
FOLLOW GENERAL DIRECTIONS ON PAGE 64.
* Layer and appliqué all rosettes together for 4 blocks.
* Reverse appliqué the red and gold slits in all pomegranates.
* Lay out all prepared appliqués on 20 1/2" squares.
* Sew finished squares together as shown on page 87.
* Sew red top and bottom borders 1" x 40 1/2" and side borders 1" x 41 1/2". Sew white top and bottom 5 1/2" x 41 1/2" borders. Add white 5 1/2" x 51 1/2" side borders.

Quilt and Bind

Templates on pages 85-89.

Continued on page 26.

Continued from page 25.

TERRY'S BERRIES
40" x 40"
INSTRUCTIONS FOR QUILT ON PAGE 24

Estimated Yardage
* 1 1/8 yd for 36 1/2" square for background — your choice
* 1/3 yd red for 2 1/2" borders
* 1/2 yd blue for 1 vase, 3 rosettes and 10 berries
* 2/3 yd red for appliqués
* 2/3 yd dark green for leaves, calyx, and small stems
* 1/3 yd light green for large center and right and left stems
* 1/3 yd yellow
* Scraps of gold

Background and Borders
SEE DIAGRAM ON PAGE 89.
* Cut 1 — 36 1/2" x 36 1/2" square.
* Cut 2 — 2 1/2" x 36 1/2" strips of red, and 2 — 2 1/2" x 40 1/2" red.

Appliqués
* Cut 1 center stem 1 1/2" X 18 1/2", green.
* A — Cut 1, reverse 1, stems, green.
* C — Cut 3 pomegranates, red.
* D — Cut 3 teardrops, gold.
* B — Cut 3 crowns, green.
* F —Cut circles, 6 yellow, 10 blue, and 8 red.
* G — Cut 1 vase, blue.
* M — Cut 3 rosettes, blue.
* E — Cut 8 leaves, green.
* O — Cut 2 calyx, green.

* P — Cut 2 buds, red.
* R — Cut 5 leaves, red.
* Y — Cut 1 rosette for signature rosette, gold.
* Z — Cut 1 rosette for signature rosette, red.
The rest of the templates are in the Rose of Sharon templates on pages 74 and 75.
* A — Cut 1 circle, red.
* C — Cut 4 large petals, red.
* D — Cut 4 petals, yellow.
* G — Cut 4 pineapples, red.
* L — Cut 12 small leaves, green.
* H — Cut 4 pineapple leaves, green.
* E — Cut 4 small calyx, red.
* K — Cut 9 leaves, green.
* N — Leaves, cut 4, reverse 4, red.
  Leaves, cut 6, reverse 6, green.
* I — Cut 8 calyx, green.
* J — Cut 8 buds, red.

Sewing Directions
REFER TO PICTURE FOR PLACEMENT.
* Appliqué all units of pomegranate, pineapples, petals, calyx, tulips, signature rosettes.
* Place vase at center bottom of square.
* Place center stem and 2 side stems.
* Cut 2 long lengths of green bias strips 1" wide for 1/2" finish stems for pineapples, tulips and signature rosette.
* Place all appliqués as shown in quilt, sew in place.
* Cut top and bottom borders, sides as shown in the diagram.

Quilt and Bind

Above: Pekin, Indiana reunion of Baker "kith and kin" including in-laws from Tash and other families. The photo was taken pre-1909 when Nell Baker moved to Oklahoma. Nell is the woman with a black neck ribbon standing in back of the sitting bearded elders. She inherited the quilt at a later date. **Right:** Log cabin of early settlers in Washington County, Indiana

Indigo Feathers and Coxcombs
87 3/4" × 87 3/4"
Unknown Maker
Collection of Terry Clothier Thompson

Unknown Maker
Indigo Feathers and Coxcombs

W ho made this quilt? Where did the maker live? Where did the pattern originate? Did one person do all the quilting? How did the maker insert the piping into those feathers? These are questions that I would like to have the answers to.

Since I do not have the past history of this quilt, I will tell its present history as I know it.

In 2007 my friend Jean Stanclift suggested we take off a day for antiquing. I was less enthusiastic than usual about finding any great quilts that day, but we went to a small Kansas town with a decent antique mall, and I started grumbling that I probably wouldn't find anything all that great, when Jean stopped me with the words "Terry, look down the aisle into that booth and check it out." All I could see was a corner of a quilt hanging on a hanger, covered with clear plastic. What I saw was a blue appliquéd feather, not green, but indigo blue with white piping sewn as the vein of the feather. I pulled it off the hanger and with Jean's help, unfolded the most unusual c. 1840-1860 appliquéd quilt I had ever seen, and I have seen a lot of quilts. Here were nine blocks of blue piped feathers, turkey red coxcomb flowers, small red birds sitting on green stems and vines on the borders. The indigo fabric has tiny, light blue dots and the turkey red is printed with small groups of three dots and one leaf. The birds, stems and leaves are solid red and green. The quilting is breathtaking, with small 14-16 stitches to the inch spaced 1/4" apart, on a startling white background. The parallel quilting lines are stitched right over the appliqués. The appliquéd coxcomb and feathers are repeated in the quilting designs. Red, 1/16" piping was placed in front of the binding.

Our friend Gail Hand drafted the quilting designs from the quilt which are included in this book for you to use when you make our own replica of *Indigo Feathers and Coxcombs*. Cheryl Harp used her camera and computer to draft the appliqué patterns. Deb Burgess chose this quilt as her contribution. She reduced the size of the patterns and made a perfect replica of the original quilt that was sewn into the feathers. Deb's quilt measures 46" x 46".

Read more of the history of piping as it relates to clothing and quilts in the directions for making *Indigo Feathers and Coxcombs*.

Indigo Feathers and Coxcombs
46" × 46"
Replica hand appliquéd and hand quilted by Debra Reimer Burgess, Inman, Kansas

Unknown Maker
Indigo Feathers and Coxcombs

87 3/4" x 87 3/4" • Instructions for quilt on page 28

Estimated Yardage
* 7 1/2 yds white for squares, borders corners and side triangles
* 1 yd indigo blue
* 3/4 yd red
* 2 1/4 yds green, for stems, leaves and border vine

Cutting
* A — Cut 18 red coxcombs.
* B — Cut 18 blue coxcomb calyx.
* C — Cut 9 indigo blue feathers.
* D — Cut 9, reverse 9 blue stems.
* E — Cut 9 rosettes, red.
* F — Cut 12 red, reverse 12 birds, red.
* G — Cut 12 green stems.
* H — Cut 24 green leaves.
* I — Cut 12 border leaves and stems.
* Cut 9 — 15 1/2" squares white for feather and coxcomb blocks.
* Cut 4 — 15 1/2" plain squares.

Sewing
* Prepare all feathers for a 1/8" reverse appliqué down the center of each.

   The maker of this vintage quilt made one block with reverse appliqué, showing the white background. Then she decided to insert white piping into the remaining 8 blocks instead of the reverse appliqué technique, which is much easier. She was familiar with the piping in the construction of c. 1850—1875 dresses. Piping was inserted into the shoulder, sleeve and skirt seams for added strength to the seam.

Setting the Quilt
See diagram on page 93.
* Sew in diagonal rows beginning in the top left corner.
* After completing all nine appliquéd blocks. Follow the figures for setting the on point blocks with the plain 15 1/2" squares, corners and side triangles.
* For the side triangles, cut 1 — 22 1/2" square into 4 triangles.
* For corner triangles, cut 2 — 11 1/2" squares.

Continued on page 32.

Continued from page 31.

BORDERS

* Cut 2 — top and bottom borders, 12 1/2" x 64 1/4"
* Cut 2 — side borders, 12 1/2" x 88 1/4".
* Appliqué the vines, birds, and stems to the borders beginning in the middle of each border, leaving the corners to be appliquéd after the borders have been sewn to the quilt. You will need the sewn corner's deep space to appliqué the vine, stem and birds.

QUILT AND BIND

Quilting this quilt will be the icing on the cake. We included the original quilting designs from the vintage quilt. We thank Gail Hand for drafting these designs for quilting.

TEMPLATES ON PAGES 90-93.

Old Mexican Rose
80" x 80"
Susannah Baer Boyer (1798-1885), Ohio; Collection of Bari Garst; Photo by Tom Pott

Susannah Baer Boyer's
Old Mexican Rose

This Mexican Rose quilt was made by Susannah Boyer for the baby she was carrying in 1844, at age 46. Susannah's own birth is documented by a German-language Fraktur that gives the date 1798, her parents' names, Jacob and Susan Baer, and the location, York County, Pennsylvania (below, right). Susannah married Jacob Boyer in 1820, and in fact, three Boyer brothers married three Baer sisters. Jacob and Susannah were early settlers in Tiffin, Ohio. Jacob was "a Lutheran, a wool carder and a dry goods merchant." Susannah gave birth to her first child, Henry in 1824, followed by Carolina Luisa, Reuben, Isaac and Mary Jane. Her sixth child was William Jacob, the baby for whom the quilt was made.

While William was growing up, a ten-year old girl named Anne E. Breese was sent by her parents on a ship from Wales to Philadelphia in the charge of her seventeen year old brother. The plan had been for Anne to live with an uncle, a circuit rider minister, but he was off preaching and didn't take care of her. A Quaker family took her in. She learned to sew buttonholes and went to work at a shoe factory partly owned by William Boyer. William and Anne married in 1872. Great-granddaughter Bari Garst credits Anne Breese Boyer with taking excellent care of the *Old Mexican Rose* quilt. In 1904, after Anne's death, William moved to Pratt, Kansas, taking the quilt with him.

Susannah's *Old Mexican Rose* is closely quilted with feathers and clamshell patterns. In one corner, the small

Right: Susannah Boyer and her son William Boyer **Below left:** Green painted willow rocking chair used by Susannah to rock her babies **Below right:** Birth certificate of Susannah Boyer, 1798.

clamshells are quilted in double lines, but it appears Susannah changed her mind and abandoned such intensive stitching in favor of clamshells of a single line throughout the rest of the quilt, a decision today's hand quilters might sympathize with.

The central portion of the quilt contains nine blocks with identical motifs, each consisting of four crossed stems; on each stem are six curved petals. The border is made up of two distinct designs. In each of the four corners is a gracefully curved vine with leaves and buds. The second design, in the middle of each side of the quilt, is made up of a red flower with a large green leaf on either side. Five circles, or berries, are placed over the flower.

Photos courtesy Bari Garst

Mexican Rose of Another Hue
80" x 80"
Hand appliquéd by Gail L. Hand, Goddard, Kansas
Machine quilted by Kim Hull, Douglass, Kansas

SUSANNAH BAER BOYER'S
OLD MEXICAN ROSE

80" x 80" • INSTRUCTIONS FOR QUILT ON PAGE 34

ESTIMATED YARDAGE
* 7 1/4 yds white or ecru
* 2 1/2 yds red
* 3 yds green
* 1/2 yd gold

CUTTING
BACKGROUND SQUARES
* Cut 9 — 20 1/2" squares.
* A — Cut 45 gold circles.
* B — Cut 216 red petals.
* C — Cut 36 large green leaves.
* Stems — Cut 18 — 1/2" X 13 1/2" green bias stems.

BORDERS
* F — Cut 4 and 4 reverse large green border leaves.
* G — Cut 20 green calyx.
* H — Cut 12 red buds and 8 gold buds.
* I — Cut 44 green leaves.
* D — Cut 4 red roses.
* E — Cut 4 green calyx.
* L — Cut 24 small green border leaves.
* J — Cut 8 green and 12 gold circles for borders.

SEWING
* Refer to the General Directions on page 64 and choose an appliqué method. Follow directions and read through all instructions before beginning to sew.
* Prepare and sew all appliqués on the 9 — 20 1/2" squares
* Cut borders. Refer to diagram on page 97.
* Appliqué, in the center of each border, the large leaf and rose.
* Sew top and bottom borders to the corner of quilt, and then sew side borders.
* Cut 4 — 1" x 28" bias strips for the vines around the corners. Use a Clover 1" bias maker for a finished 1/2" wide vine.
* Fold long bias vine in half and pin center of vine in the corners of quilt. Lay out the curves as seen in the picture.
* Place finished buds H and large leaves I along vine as shown.
* Place small leaves L underneath buds.

QUILT AND BIND

TEMPLATES ON PAGES 94-97.

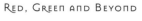

Christmas Cactus
84" × 84"
Catherine Johnson Cover (1830-1888)
Pennsylvania
Collection of Martha Jo Longhofer

CATHERINE JOHNSON COVER'S
CHRISTMAS CACTUS

Catherine
Johnson Cover
Courtesy of
Martha Jo
Longhofer

In 1881 in Fayette County, Pennsylvania, Mary Elizabeth Cover married George Wesley Easter. The couple traveled by train to Kansas to farm a claim eight miles south of Abilene. Mary Elizabeth, or Libby, had a red and green appliqué quilt made by her mother, Catherine Johnson Cover. The quilt was a symbol of the bond between mother and daughter and would be a link between the Easters' Pennsylvania roots and yet unborn Kansas generations.

The woman who made the quilt, Catherine Johnson Cover, was the daughter of a Scottish-Swiss father and a German mother. She married John Newcomer Cover in 1855. and Mary Elizabeth was one of five children in the Cover family.

After Mary Elizabeth and George Easter moved to Kansas, her father wrote in a letter dated December 12, 1883: "...Mary Liby we received your letter on the 11th of Dec we was glad to hear from you from reading your letter we belief you are some homesick this we expected if you did not you would be very different from other people we would like to see you and George come home sometime when it suits you best. now Lib I want you to make yourself as happy as you can I think you have a great country and I think you are getting along faster there than you could here in PA." Libby made only two trips back to her home in Pennsylvania.

Martha Jo Longhofer, granddaughter of the Easters, believes that since her grandparents reared a family of nine children, the quilt would have been worn out had it not been given special care and 'saved.' "My grandmother [Mary Elizabeth Easter]

Reminiscences of Lucetta Johnson, niece of Catherine Johnson Cover, writing of her grandparents (Catherine's parents):

Peter and Barbara Honsaker Johnson lived on a farm in Jacobs Creek, Fayette Co., PA. He had a flour mill and a saw mill and built a foundry where they made heating and cooking stoves, plows, kettles, pots and skillets. The parents of thirteen children, they were good natured and tolerant and enjoyed the fun almost as much as their children. Special on the farm were husking bees, butchering, barn raisings, sugar making, quiltings, harvesting. Entertainment during the winter evenings consisted of sleighing parties, singing school, spelling matches. But best of all there were evenings at home where by the light of candles, Barbara Johnson and her daughters sat knitting and piecing quilts while Peter and the boys read.

left all of her family to come to Kansas at the age of 23, so if her mother made and gave her the quilt, it was no doubt very dear to her."

Catherine's Christmas Cactus is a four-block quilt. Small, medium, and large rosettes make up the center of each block. From the center rosette, a stylized feathery leaf with a flower bud at the end reaches out to each corner. Reverse applique on the leaves allows an orange color to show through, giving the leaf more definition. Between the large leaves is a calyx with three plumes facing right and three facing left. One leaf, one plume, and one bud make up the border patterns. The quilting is in parallel lines and feathering.

Left: Mary Elizabeth Cover and John Wesley Easter; Courtesy of Martha Jo Longhofer

Christmas Cactus Pillow Quilt
20" × 20"
Machine appliquéd by
RoRi Matters Stoller,
Overland Park, Kansas

Catherine Johnson Cover's
Christmas Cactus

88" x 88" • Instructions for quilt on page 38

Estimated Yardage

* 7 1/4 yds white/ecru for 4 — 32 1/2" squares, and 4 borders
* 3 1/4 yds green — for leaves, calyx, rosettes in blocks, and leaves in borders
* 2 1/2 yds red — for petals and rosette B
* 1/2 yd gold for reverse appliqué strips under leaves and 4 gold rosettes

Cutting Blocks and Borders

* Cut 4 — 32 1/2" squares.
* Cut 16 strips of 1 1/4" x 8 1/4" for reverse appliqué in leaf E gold.
* A — Cut 4 circles, green.
* B — Cut 4 small rosettes, gold.
* C— Cut 4 medium rosettes, red.
* D — Cut 4 large rosettes, green.
* E — Cut 16 large leaves, green.
* F — Cut 30 large petals and 30 reverse, red.
* G — Cut 30 medium red petals and 30 reverse.
* H — Cut 30 small petals and 30 reverse, red.
* I — Cut 30 buds for leaves in blocks and borders, red.
* J — Cut 14 leaves for leaves in borders, green.
* L — Cut 30 calyx and stems for blocks and borders, green.
* M — Cut 16 strips for reverse appliqué in leaf J, gold.

Sewing Blocks and Borders

* Layer and sew the 3 rosettes and center circle-A-B-C-D, for 4 blocks.
* Prepare all large leaves E & J for reverse appliqué. Baste gold strip under cut line, turn edge of slit, turn under 1/4" seam allowance and sew in place.
* Find center of 32 1/2" squares, place sewn rosettes in center of each square. Pin all pattern pieces and baste in place.
* Appliqué each block, then set into a four-block square. See diagram on page 101.
* Cut 2 top and bottom borders, 12 1/2" x 64 1/2". Cut 2 side borders, 12 1/2" x 88 1/2".
* Place the border leaf, calyx, petals, and buds. Refer to diagram for placement.
* Appliqué each border.
* Sew borders to quilt.

Quilt and Bind

Templates on pages 98-101.

Right: Woman at sewing machine, circa 1853.

Rose Tree
76" × 76"
Adriana (Agnes) Holtgraver
Kansas, c. 1935
Collection of Donald W Holtgraver, Sr. and Ann Holtgraver

Adriana "Agnes" Porsch Holtgraver's
Rose Tree

Agnes Holtgraver's family did not know this quilt existed until after her death in 1984, so a certain amount of mystery surrounds it. Agnes was born in 1914 and raised in Olpe, Kansas, a small German, Catholic community nine miles south of Emporia. Although named 'Adriana' after a grandmother, she was known all her life as 'Agnes.' She was the daughter of William and Emma Bolz Porsch. Three of her grandparents migrated from Germany; the grandmother named Adriana was from Holland. Agnes had three brothers and four sisters. In 1941 the Porsch family moved to Olathe, Kansas. Agnes married Oscar Holtgraver and raised two sons.

On the quilt inherited by Agnes's family, quilting stitches that range from eleven to eighteen stitches per inch suggest that it was probably quilted by several people, or a group. The family wonders if Agnes might have quilted with her four sisters: Bertha, Gertrude, Martha and Rose.

The appliquéd motif in the five on-point blocks is a stem with three roses and many leaves. The arrangement of the flowers, leaves and stems is asymmetrical, making it more naturalistic than the symmetrical, stylized look of most 19th Century appliqué quilts. Although the quilt used blue for the stems, leaves, and sashing, rather than green, it could be said to have been made in the 'red and green style.'

Agnes Holtgraver
Courtesy of Donald W. Holtgraver, Jr.

Rose Tree was the only 20th Century quilt selected for this book. The proximity of Olpe to Emporia might be significant. Given the sophisticated appliqué pattern and the fine quality of the quilting stitches, it would be reasonable to think that Agnes and her sisters may have been influenced by the exceptional quilts made by a group of women in Emporia between 1925 and 1950.

In her later life, Agnes quilted at the 'morning Grange' in the town of Gardner.

Rose Tree
72" × 72"
Machine appliquéd and machine quilted by Susan Martin, Olathe, Kansas

Agnes Holtgraver's
Rose Tree

76" x 76" • Instructions for quilt on page 42

Agnes stepped out of the red and green traditional look and chose to color the leaves, stems, calyx and sashing a beautiful blue color. Her unique roses and buds are sewn with the turkey red and pink solid colors — not a trace of green anywhere. The choice of blue over green was not that common in 19th Century appliquéd quilts, but blue does appear occasionally.

The *Rose Tree* quilt contains 5 blocks set on point. Corner squares are cut 25 1/2" X 25 1/2" and each have a 2 1/2" sashing for a finished measurement of 29". The center square does not have a sash, and is cut 29 1/2", to finish the 29" square.

Agnes pieced the numbered "F" petals, so you might enjoy a different approach to creating the petals, or make a template of the petals into one round shape and appliqué it to the pink rose circles.

Estimated Yardage

* 5 1/2 yds for 6 blocks, corner and side triangles, white or ecru
* 3 1/4 yds blue for sashing around blocks and bias stems, leaves and center stems
* 1/2 yd pink for roses
* 1/2 yd red for rose petals and buds

Cutting

For 5 background blocks, cut 1 — 29 1/2" square, and 4 — 25 1/2" squares, white or ecru

* A — Cut 19 circles of pink.
* B — Cut 19 large petals, red.
* C — Cut 19, reverse 19 red petals.
* D — Cut 19, reverse 19 red petals.
* F — Cut 19 each of #'s 1, 2, 3, 4, 5, and 6 petals, red.
* G – large bud #1 — Cut 10 red for blocks and 8 red for large triangles.

* O — small bud #2 — Cut 10 red for blocks and 12 red for large triangles and corners.
* H — Cut blue leaves: 125 for 5 blocks, 24 for corners, and 68 for setting triangles = a total of 217 blue leaves. All stems, leaves, and calyx are blue.
* I — Cut 18, reverse 18 calyx #1, blue.
* J — Cut 9, reverse 5 stems, blue.
* K — Cut 40 calyx, blue.
* M — Cut 18 blue stems for large calyx, reverse 4 for small calyx.
* N — Cut 18, reverse 18 blue stems for large calyx.
* Q — Cut 18, reverse 4, blue calyx for small bud O.

Sewing

* Refer to the General Directions and Good Advice section on page 64 for guidance on cutting and sewing.
* Appliqué all B-C-D-E petals to the 19 large pink circle A.
* Appliqué or piece the outside ring of petals F to the pink rose center A.
* For the center of each rose, embroider 12 French knots.
* Sew the #1 and #2 buds to calyx I and Q.
* Add the stems M and N behind bud #1, and M behind bud #2.
* Sew the calyx K to large bud I and small bud Q.
* Cut 1" strips of bias for the center bias stems and 1/2" strips of bias for the smaller bud's stems.
* Using the *Rose Tree* photo, lay out the appliqués with the 5 blocks on point referring to the picture and diagram for guidance.

Continued on page 46.

Continued from page 45.

* For the 4 side setting triangles, cut one 42 1/4" square — refer to figure #1 on page 104 — and cut into 4 triangles.
* For the 4 corner triangles, cut 2 — 21 3/8" squares. Refer to figure #2.
* Appliqué the side and corner triangles as shown in the photograph.
* The side setting triangles have 1 rose, 1 large bud and 1 small bud. The corner triangles have 1 large bud and 2 small buds.

Rose Tree quilting detail by Susan Martin

Sashing and Setting Finished Blocks

* Cut 16 — 2 1/2" x 25 1/2" crossgrain strips of blue for the sashing for 4 corner blocks. Refer to diagram for sewing sashing to squares. The center square has no sashing.
* Set appliquéd corners, blocks, side triangles on the diagonal, as shown in diagram.

Quilt and Bind

Templates on pages 102–105.

Flowers from Winnie
79" × 84"
Winnie Piper Groninger (1811-1897)
Indiana
Collection of Mary Louise Newcomb Heaton

Winnie Piper Groninger's
Flowers from Winnie

These words were written on a scrap of paper found attached to the quilting frame of Mary Emma Groninger Tryon. The sentiments expressed would seem to apply to her grandmother, the woman who made this lovely quilt. Winnie Piper was born in 1811 in Ohio, the daughter of Philip Piper and Elizabeth Minear. In 1831 Winnie married Pennsylvanian Leonard Groninger, and the couple went to live in Wabash County, Indiana. Seven children were born to this union, but only one son, Henry Lewis Groninger, survived to adulthood. After Leonard's death in 1871, Winnie made her home with Henry, his wife Rebecca, and their family of ten children: six sons and four daughters. Winnie gave a quilt to each of her granddaughters, Loa, Mary Emma, her namesake Winnie, and Iva Rebecca. The quilt with the baskets of tulips was brought to Pawnee County, Kansas in 1882 by her second granddaughter, Mary Emma Tryon.

Some of the appliquéd flower pieces in Winnie's quilt remain a strong turkey red; others have faded to a soft rose color. Each of the four bouquets of tulips is placed in a green container. Each has a center stem holding a tulip. On both sides of the stem are two more stems of tulips and two developing buds. The on-point placement of the four baskets forms a large center space that is filled with crossed stems of tulips. Curved-stem sprays of flowers and leaves fill the four corners, and straight stems with flowers are mid-point on each side of the quilt. The quilt's border is a scalloped swag of red, green and chrome orange, with an appliquéd bud in each scallop. Quilting is in a one-inch square grid over the entire surface of the quilt, including over the appliquéd designs.

The Groninger farm in Indiana.
Courtesy of Mary Louise Newcomb Heaton

Basket of Tulips
52" × 52"
Hand appliquéd and hand quilted, using their own hand dyed fabrics,
by Joan Bruce, Barbara Collins, Rene Jennings, Andi Perejda,
Arroyo Grande, California

Flowers from Winnie

83 1/2" x 83 1/2" • Instructions for quilt on page 48

Yardage

* 7 yds white or ecru for 5 blocks, corners, setting triangles and borders.
* 3 yds of red, and 2/3 yd dark red
* 3 1/2 yds of green
* 1 1/2 yds of cheddar yellow or gold

Cutting blocks and borders

* A — Cut 4 vase bottoms, green.
* B — Cut 4 vase tops, red.
* C — Cut 20, reverse 20 petals red for blocks. Cut 20, reverse 20 green for border.
* D — Cut 20 petals for large tulips, gold. Cut 10 red and 10 gold for border.
* E — Cut 40, reverse 40 petals for blocks and borders, green.
* F — Cut 40 small buds for blocks, red.
* M — Cut 40 small bud calyx, green.
* G — Cut 4 leaves, gold, for middle 22" square.
* H — Cut 16 petals, dark red, for setting triangles.
* I — Cut 16 medium petals, red.
* J — For small medium leaf J:
  Cut 20 green for border tulip.
  Cut 56 green for baskets, cut 32 gold for side triangles.
  Cut 48 green for side triangles.
* K — Cut 16 small petals, dark red, for corner triangles.
* L — Cut 16 buds, red, for corner triangles.
* N — Cut 4 large petals, medium red, for center square.
* O — Cut 4 large buds, gold, for petal N.
* P — Cut 22 gold /cheddar border swags.
* Q — Cut 22 green border swags.
* R — Cut 22 red border swags.
* S — Cut 8 leaves, green, for center square.

* 5 basket blocks:
  Cut 5 — 23" squares of background fabric
  Cut 2 — 10 1/2" x 64" top and bottom borders
  Cut 2 — 10 1/2" x 84" side borders

Sewing

* Refer to picture of quilt and focus on 1 block for placing the prepared appliqué pieces. All 5 blocks are on point, so lay out the basket, center and side stems, tulips, buds and leaves. Note the center block used different leaves and tulip size.
* Cut 2-3 long 1" strips for 1/2" green stems and vines. Use a 1/2" Clover bias maker to turn 1" strip into 1/2" stems.
* Place 5 – 23" blocks on point. Press a vertical and a diagonal line on each square, as a guide for placing stems. Place the top tulip in the top corner of the 4 squares. Place the basket in the lower corner of the squares, referring to picture. Lay long center stems down the center from the tulip to the basket. Now place right and left from basket lid. Follow picture for for laying out the rest of the stems and tulips. Repeat this process for the center block, 4 side triangles, and 4 corner triangles for placement for all stems and tulips. Fill in spaces with leaves, buds, and stems as shown.
* Cut 1 – 33" square and cut on both diagonals for 4 setting triangles.
* Cut 2 – 16 3/4" squares and cut on one diagonal for 4 corner triangles.

Continued on page 52.

Continued from page 51.

✳ Place appliqués and stems, referring to the photo. Baste and appliqué all block's corners, and side setting triangles.

✳ After center blocks, side and corner triangles are appliquéd, set on the diagonal. See diagram.

✳ Cut top and bottom borders 10 1/2" x 64 1/2".

✳ Cut side borders 10 1/2" x 84 1/2".

✳ Piece 22 swags R-P-Q. Piece border tulips.

✳ Place swags on each border referring to picture. Top and bottom borders have 5 swags, and side borders have 4 swags, wtih 1 swag in each corner. Appliqué tulips and stems to top end of each swag.

✳ Sew appliqué top and bottom borders to quilt. Sew the side borders. See diagram. Appliqué corner swags into the corners of the quilt.

Quilt and Bind

Templates on pages 106-109.

GALLERY

Coxcombs
72" × 81"
Alice Rose Smith Klein
Indiana, c. 1870; State Historical Society of Iowa, Des Moines

Black Beauty 2
82" x 83"
Machine appliquéd by Barb Fife, Overland Park, Kansas,
and machine quilted by Sandy Gore, Liberty, Missouri

Cherry Baskets
48" x 48"
Hand appliquéd and hand quilted by
Nancy Hornback, Wichita, Kansas

Red and Green, Past and Present
76" x 76"
Designed by Terry Thompson, Lawrence, Kansas
Appliquéd by Jean Stanclift, Lawrence, Kansas, and quilted by Lori Kukuk, McLouth, Kansas
Appliqué designs from *Quilts in Red and Green*

Mexican Rose
26 1/2" × 26 1/2"
Hand appliquéd and quilted by Ilyse Moore, Overland Park, Kansas

Black Beauty 1
82" x 83"
Appliquéd by Barb Fife, quilted by Sandy Gore, Liberty, Missouri
Patterns from *Quilts in Red and Green*

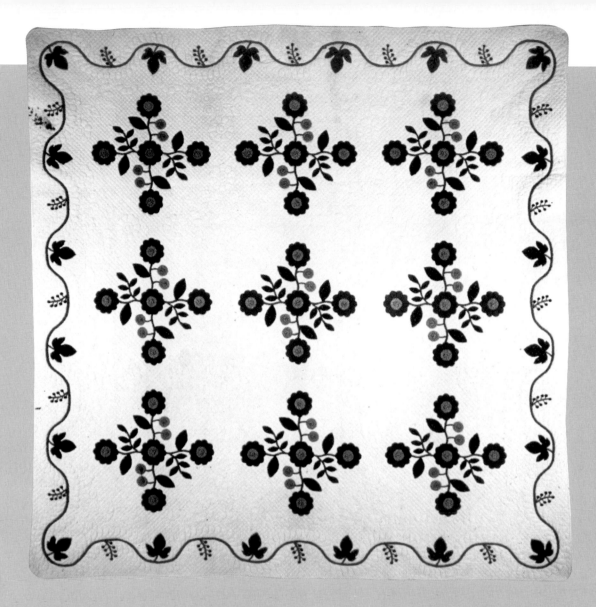

About Democrat Rose

In our 2006 publication, *Quilts in Red and Green*, we told of a woman from Emporia, Kansas, who copied a mid-19th Century quilt made in Ohio by Isabel Wilson. We noted that the copied quilt won a first prize at the Kansas State Fair, and we wondered if this copier might have been one of the "famed Emporia quiltmakers." And, indeed it was. Soon after, we came across the copied version in an exhibit at the Kansas Museum of History. It was made by Josephine Craig, a contemporary of the well-known quiltmaker Rose Kretsinger in the 1930s.

There is more to this story. The owner of the original *Rose Appliqué* quilt, a great-niece of Isabel Wilson, lived in Greensburg, Kansas. On May 4, 2007, a tornado destroyed the entire town of Greensburg. We have since learned that the quilt survived but was irreparably damaged — heart-rending to those of us who love the old red and green quilts. But it is a comfort to know that Isabel Wilson's beautiful quilt will continue to inspire and give pleasure to 21st Century quiltmakers and beyond.

Democrat Rose
Made by Josephine Craig, c. 1935, Collection of the Kansas Museum of History. This is an almost exact copy of Isabel Wilson's quilt, except for the blue centers of the flower buds that are pink in the original.

Christmas Cactus block
20" × 20"
Machine appliquéd by Jean Stanclift, Lawrence, Kansas

Comments From and About
The Quiltmakers

RoRi Stoller
Christmas Cactus Pillow Quilt

"This Project was fun and easy."

RoRi is new to quilting and she has sewn some lovely quilts. Her pillow quilt is very creative and the pattern was challenging. Rori and my son Shawn grew up together. — *Terry Thompson*

Barb Nickelson
Starburst Buds and Berries

I've finished work on the appliqué for the Buds and Berries quilt, and I'm excited! Here is a tip for easier appliqué, without stretching the bias edges of setting triangles. Cut the square and press the diagonals, but leave the piece uncut. Do the appliqué on the square (no bias edges to stretch out of shape), and when the appliqué is complete, cut on the diagonals. "Thanks for the opportunity."

Cheryl Harp
Red and Green Jubilee

From the moment Nancy and Terry showed me the photographs of the Mary Turley and Alice Smith quilts I knew I had to make my own. For me it was the perfect red and green quilt. I drafted the block to imitate the grace and extra details in Alice Smith's quilt. The touch of whimsy from Mary Turley's border was the inspiration for my border.

By nature I am a very precise needle turn appliqué quilter. I also find great pleasure in prepared and machine appliqué. My greatest joy in any appliqué is the process of taking little bits of fabric, sticking them together, and going around stitch by stitch till I have a beautiful bouquet or wreath. Whether you are working by hand or machine you develop a rhythm that is relaxing and satisfying.

Gail L. Hand
Mexican Rose of a Different Hue

I grew up in New Hampshire and learned to sew from both my mother and grandmother. My grandmother lived next door and was a wool inspector in the local woolen mill. I learned from them to spend lots of time laying out patterns, matching plaids, etc. before cutting and sewing. (I still have a wool lined suit my

mother and I made in the early sixties). Now I can hardly get around to mending clothes, let alone sew clothes. I also rarely finish projects. I would much rather collect a finished antique quilt — it's faster than sewing and appliquéing. I do, however, enjoy the process of hand appliqué and the visual imagery of color and design that is created within the appliqué. It is very portable and keeps me happy and relaxed and I don't have to finish everything.

Left: Cheryl Harp; **Above, inset:** Gail Hand

Clockwise from top:
Marlene Royce; Deb
Burgess; Kim Hull;
and Susan Martin.

Marlene Royse
Shadows of the Past

My favorite method of machine appliqué is a blend of techniques. I prepare the appliqué pieces using heat-resistant template plastic and spray starch to turn the edges under. I use the machine vari-overlock stitch and size 100 silk thread in matching colors provides an almost invisible stitch, which is easily mistaken for hand appliqué.

Susan Martin
Rose Tree

For machine appliqué, use a matching thread on top, and a thread that matches the background fabric in the bobbin. Set the machine to do a small zigzag stitch. The needle needs to catch the background and the appliqué piece. This quilt was appliquéd using prepared appliqué shapes. This involves using a washable glue stick to turn the edges of the fabric to the back side of the foundation material. Sign and date your quilt!

Mindy Peterson
Midnight Garden Memories

This quilt is made with only four fabrics. I used a black tone on tone for the background, a bright green for the stems and leaves, a bright pink for the flowers and pineapples and a bright yellow for the flowers. The black background provides a striking contrast to the bright fabrics used for the appliqué. Look for Mindy's new pattern company, "5acre Designs"

Kim Hull (right) worked on *Mexican Rose of Another Hue.*

Deb Burgess
Indigo Feathers and Coxcombs

I am privileged to have a strong quilting heritage which includes my grandmother, mother, several aunts and my sister. Growing up, there were always quilts on the beds at our house, and because of that, quilts are a symbol of home, comfort, and family to me. I especially enjoy working with vintage fabrics and traditional patterns, and often find myself in awe of quilters from the past and the beautiful quilts which they created without all the advantages that we have today in tools, fabrics, and lighting.

Joan Bruce
Basket of Tulips

Joan specializes in piecing, and computer generated fabric design. She has transferred her fine art work to fabric.

Barbara Collins
Basket of Tulips

Barbara prefers appliqué, but is proficient in many types of quilting. She has won local prizes for her work. Memoir writing is her other passion.

Rene Jennings
Basket of Tulips

Rene is a fabric artist, and teacher with proficiency in all types of quilting. She has made a number of award winning quilts and appeared on "Simply Quilts."

Lori Kukuk worked on *Midnight Garden Memories* and *Red and Green, Past and Present.*

Clockwise from top: Lori Kukuk; Barb Fife with her family; Ilyse Moore

Andi Perejda
Basket of Tulips

Andi is an NQA certified judge who also teaches workshops, including appliqué, hand quilting and "Circle of Illusion." She has won many awards for her quilts, including Merit Hand Quilting at IQA, McCall's Hand Workmanship Award at AQS, Best of Show and Appliqué Master at the Appliqué Society Show and First in Art Quilts at both NQA and Houston. She has also appeared on "Simply Quilts." Her gallery of quilts can be viewed at WWW.andiperejda.com

The Basket of Tulips group has collaborated on other quilts.

Ilyse Moore
Mexican Rose

Although I have always loved quilts, I did not start quilting until 2000 after I had retired from teaching. I took beginning quilting and appliqué classes and discovered I also loved making quilts. However, I want to do it all, but I realize that time, money, and talent will not allow me to make at least one of every quilt style I like. My compromise is to miniaturize the quilts I make. In this way I can make tops and hand quilt small quilts of many quilting traditions.

Quilting tips:

1. Remember quilting is your hobby. If your project is frustrating you, do something else for a while.

2. Most of my quilts are half size. The blocks are small, but not so tiny that the project becomes very difficult.

Yes, I do make large quilts, too. Most are given away, but I am getting a rather large collection of quilts that I cannot bear to part with.

Barb Fife
Black Beauty 1, Black Beauty 2

I made the 2 quilts using batik fabrics. I chose solid black for the background and bright colors of reds, pinks, and greens for the flowers and stems. I fused the pieces to the background and then buttonhole stitched them with a rayon Isacord thread. I use a stitch length of 2mm. and width of 2mm. I like the sheen that the rayon thread gives the finished product. The first quilt, BLACK BEAUTY, won Best of Show at the Johnson County, Kansas Fair in July, 2006.

General Directions
(Using a coxcomb and currant pattern as an example)

READ THROUGH ALL DIRECTIONS
BEFORE BEGINNING.

✳ Prewash all fabrics.

✳ We are using a coxcomb pattern as an example. Add 1/4" seam allowance as you cut out the appliqués. To begin, prepare the background block by cutting a 20 1/2" square. Remember, fabric is 40-45" wide so you will get 2 blocks per cut.

✳ Fold square in half, then in half again.

✳ Lightly press on folded lines. Then fold square on the diagonal and press diagonal lines. These folded/pressed lines serve as a placement guide for the appliqués.

✳ To prepare appliqués, cut a template of each appliqué. You may stack your fabric and cut several layers at once, but you will need to draw around the template on each piece to give you a pencil "turn under" line.

✳ Draw around templates on the right side of the fabric. Cut out 1/4" from pencil line as no seam allowance has been added to the patterns. Cut one color at a time.

✳ Historically all appliqués are laid out on the background block, pinned and basted in place, using the pressed lines as a guide. Before this step is taken, however, appliqué the flower or center rosette units together before placing them on a block. It is much easier to

sew smaller units together separately than on the block.

✳ Now lay out all prepared appliqués, following the pressed lines as a guide. Beginning in the center, pin and baste 1/2" from the raw edge, remove pins and appliqué in place, tucking under the ends of stems and leaves a good 1/4" - 1/2" so raw edges do not appear as you sew.

✳ Now the sewing part: I strongly suggest that beginners appliqué in the top running stitch, even pre-basting the appliqués before pinning and basting to the block. This just means that all raw edges of the appliqués are turned under on the pencil line 1/4" and basted. This prepares the edges ahead of appliquéing. Yes, it is an extra step, but the beginner has greater success and will love to appliqué. Of course as one improves this step may be eliminated; however, I still pre-baste if several units are to be layered.

* Intermediate and advanced appliquérs may use the blind stitch or machine appliqué using freezer paper techniques. Consult your local quilt shop or quilt guild for appliqué classes, learn all the techniques, then choose what is best for you. In taking a class, you will learn so much more about appliqué techniques, and you will be supporting your shop or guild at the same time.

* Do not cut out behind appliqués, as the appliqués need the support of the background block. (You will have to cut backs out when using the freezer paper technique to remove the paper.)

* Set finished blocks.

* Set blocks on square or on point.

* Borders: I do not miter borders. I sew the top and bottom first, then the sides.

* Find the center of the border and swag. Center swag at center of border, then everything is laid out from center.

* Appliqué borders separately from blocks, then sew to body of quilt placing corner swags to meet the two connecting borders.

* Remove all basting.

* To quilt, use background filler patterns for the empty spaces between blocks, such as clamshell, double lines, feathers, or diamonds. Any design will look terrific on these quilts.

Marking Your Quilt

* Trace the quilt patterns on to your quilt top by placing the top over the printed pattern, then lightly draw with a #2 pencil over the lines or make small dots. If the pattern lines are too light to show through the quilt fabric, darken the patterns with a black marker. Tops may also be marked from the top with commercial plastic templates. Straight lines and grids may be marked with a yardstick. Use a #2 lead pencil. It will usually fade away as you quilt or with the first or second washing, if lines are not too dark. If your fabric is dark, you can create a light table by using a storm window propped between two chairs with a lamp underneath to illuminate the design. Trace, using a white lead dressmaker's pencil or art pencil.

Continued on page 66.

Continued from page 65.

Quilting

✻ Place backing (wrong side up), batting, the quilt top (right side up), on a flat surface. Pin and baste all three layers together, smoothing out wrinkles. Arrange the quilt in hoop. Start in center, working toward the edge, using a single thread and knot, bringing needle through all three layers from underneath side of quilt. Pop the knot through the back layer, thereby securing the knot in the batting layer. Now you are ready to quilt. With the needle at a 45-degree angle, take small running stitches, catching all three layers. To finish off, run the needle under the top layer of the quilt the length of the needle, then trim off the extra thread. (For more information about appliqué, refer to Terry's book, *Four Block Quilts* from *The Kansas City Star* at your quilt shop.)

✻ Bind edges. (I like to make a bias binding.) Attach a sleeve. Sign and date your quilt, and you are finished.

✻ To cut out 9 - 20 1/2" background squares, leave yardage folded to cut 20 1/2" squares 2 square blocks at a time. This includes the seam allowance.

✻ Cut borders on the cross grain and piece end to end.

Coxcomb & Currant Directions
as an Example

✻ Follow General Directions above for preparation of background block and appliqué pieces.

✻ Appliqué small rosette A to large center flower B.

✻ Appliqué calyx C to middle coxcomb D to top coxcomb E.

✻ Match center of large rosette A-B to center of background block. Pin in place.

✻ Pin stem F on horizontal and vertical lines. Pin coxcomb units on horizontal and vertical lines, covering the raw edge of stem.

✻ To reverse appliqué centers of ferns, cut a slit down the center of each fern on the dotted line shown on the pattern piece. Cut fabric for the insert approximately 3" x 11 1/2". (The shape has been outlined on the pattern piece.) DO NOT skimp on this insert piece as you want all raw edges of the slash to disappear onto the insert, and not come up short. Sew insert before basting to block. Appliqué berries H to insert. You may have the background show instead of adding an insert as shown in the quilt.

✻ Pin ferns G on the diagonal lines, referring to the photo for placement.

✻ Baste all pieces in place.

✻ Remove pins and appliqué.

✻ Sew the blocks together.

✻ Quilt and bind.

Good Advice
Appliqué techniques

i. Top running stitch appliqué

✻ Many antique quilts were sewn with a running stitch to secure the appliqué. This basic hand-sewing stitch, the one we use for quilting and piecing, is the easiest hand appliqué stitch. I recommend this technique for beginning appliqué artists because the stitches can be easily seen on the top of the appliqué. The stitch is speedy and you may take three to four stitches at a time. Although this technique flattens the appliqué somewhat, it is secure and gives a finished look. A different colored thread can add a little color or a strong outline to your appliqué.

✷ Prepare the appliqué by placing the pattern on the top side of the fabric. Trace around the appliqué with a #2 lead pencil. If the fabric is dark, use a chalk pencil. This line is the guideline for turning under the 1/4" seam allowance.

✷ Cut, adding 1/4" seam allowance around the pencil line.

✷ I recommend that beginners pre-baste each appliqué piece by turning under the 1/4" seam on the pencil line and basting the edges over. Baste all appliqué patches to the background, tucking under points and raw edges.

✷ Stitch, gathering your fabric up on your needle as you go, about 1/16 - 1/8" from the edge of the appliquéd piece. You don't want to do a stab stitch (one stitch at a time).

✷ Use contrasting thread to show your even stitches.

ii. Blind stitch

✷ Pin and baste each layer of the design in place. Knot a thread and bring your needle from the wrong side of the background block and through the folded edge of the appliqué. Take needle back down thru block and back up again about 1/16" from the last stitch into the fold of the appliqué. Use your needle to turn under the raw edge, press with your finger and hold in place with your thumb. I move my thumb and finger press about 1" ahead of my last stitch. (Finger press 1/2" ahead of the last stitch, using needle to turn under raw edge of appliqué.) This technique gives a rounded "lifted" edge to the appliqué.

Making berries and currants

✷ To make berries and currants (or any round shape), use sticky removable labels found at office supply stores for large, medium and small circles. Place sticky labels on fabric, cut 1/4" seam allowance and glue or hand baste the edges under. Remove labels and appliqué.

Colors and Fabric

Colors

The traditional colors of red, green, pink, chrome yellow, and orange — better known as cheddar, appear in the 19th century appliquéd quilts. Because of their special status, women saved them for special occasions, thus sparing the quilts from hard use and harsh laundry methods. However, after 150 years, some quilts show wear and the reds in particular turn a nice shade of pink. The early turkey red calico could be a blue red or a tomato red shade. In Pennsylvania, quilters substituted a cinnamon red calico for the brighter turkey reds of the period.

If you prefer a historical look for your antique bedroom furniture, choose the traditional red. If you want a quilt that fits into your more conventional decorating style, choose a nice combination of pinks and a variety of light greens. Barb Fife chose black as a background for her shaded batik fabrics.

As for greens, you may choose the traditional bright, spring greens that look like the early greens, or tone down the shades that look good with the pink calicos. Use these greens with the cinnamon reds and pinks for the Pennsylvania German madder in your quilts. Many women used a lovely teal blue in place of green. Blue was not often used, but was not all that uncommon. Mary Parks Lawrence's *Cherry Basket* quilt is a good example of a teal green.

Use pink and yellow and cheddar as accent colors, for buds, rosettes, vases, and berries. Background blocks were a light muslin or white, sometimes a shirting. A small print looks nice also. It's very sweet for a girl's bedroom.

Fabric

Estimated yardage for a 9-block sampler quilt with borders

* For the sampler quilt blocks, choose a nice variety of reds, greens, and accent colors of pink, cheddar, yellow, and gold. I prefer to mix different shades of the main colors for a less formal quilt.

I suggest you buy:

* 1/2 to 3/4 yards of 3 or 4 different shades of red and green for a real scrappy look, which is more contemporary. If you prefer to use one fabric for each of the red and green, buy at least 2 1/2 to 3 yards of red, and 3 yards of green for bias stems, leaves and border vines. Buy 1 1/2 yards of your accent colors of pink, yellow, cheddar, or gold.

For a 9 — 20" block with 10 1/2" borders, buy:

* 7 1/4 yards. Cut borders on the cross grain. For 2 1/2" wide finished sashing, buy 2 yards. Backing fabric for an 86" x 105" quilt with 9 1/2" borders takes 7 1/4 yards.

* The average size of each vintage quilt is 85" x 90", so I estimated the yardage for the backgrounds of blocks, borders, appliqués and backings/binds. These are traditional colors. Choose your favorite colors for your home.

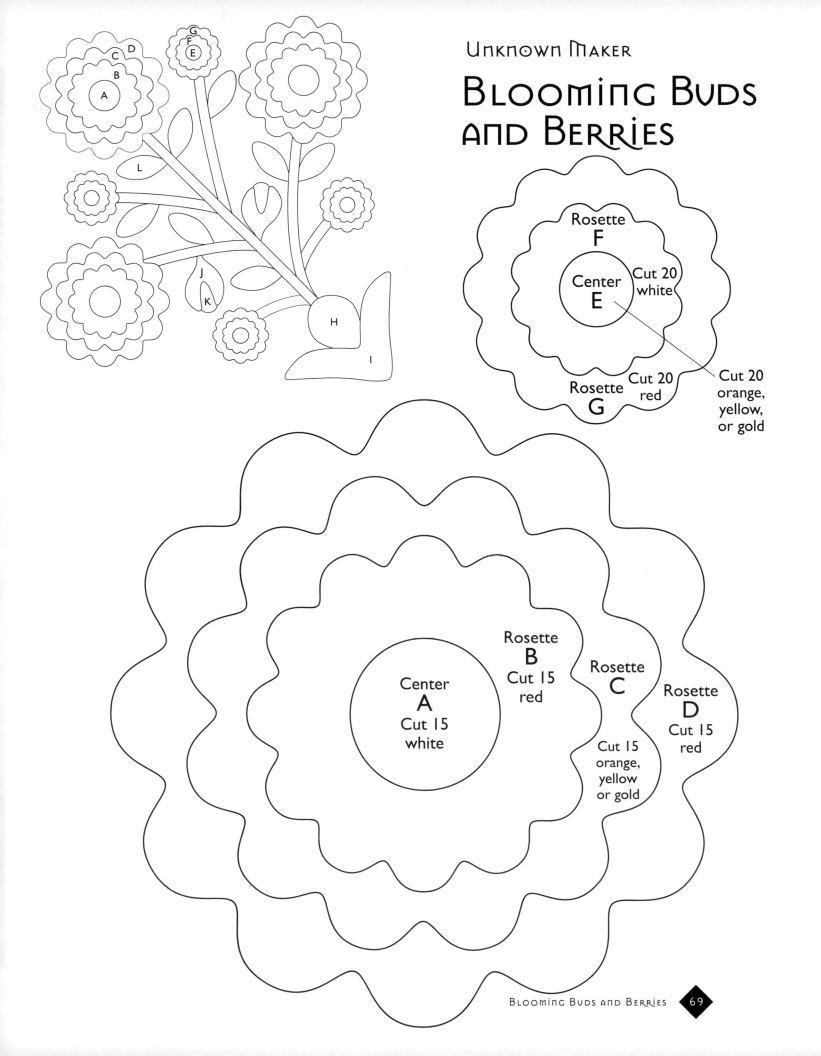

Blooming Buds and Berries

Rosette
F

Center
E

Cut 20
white

Cut 20
red

Rosette
G

Cut 20
orange,
yellow,
or gold

Rosette
B
Cut 15
red

Rosette
C

Rosette
D
Cut 15
red

Center
A
Cut 15
white

Cut 15
orange,
yellow
or gold

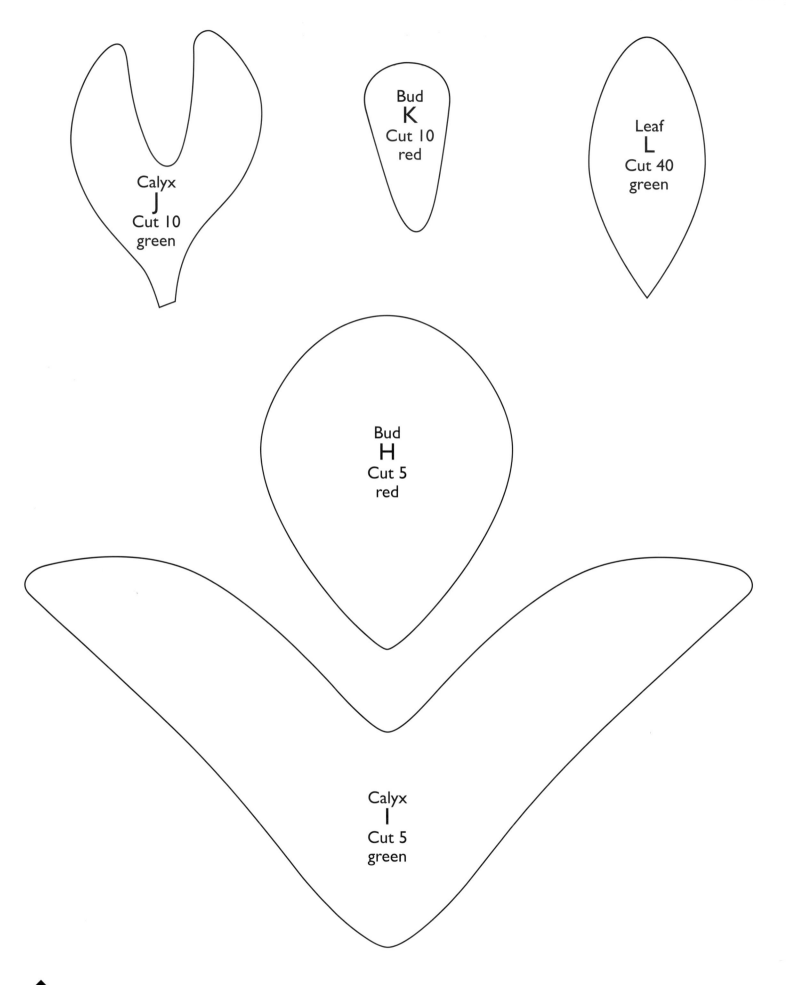

Calyx
J
Cut 10
green

Bud
K
Cut 10
red

Leaf
L
Cut 40
green

Bud
H
Cut 5
red

Calyx
I
Cut 5
green

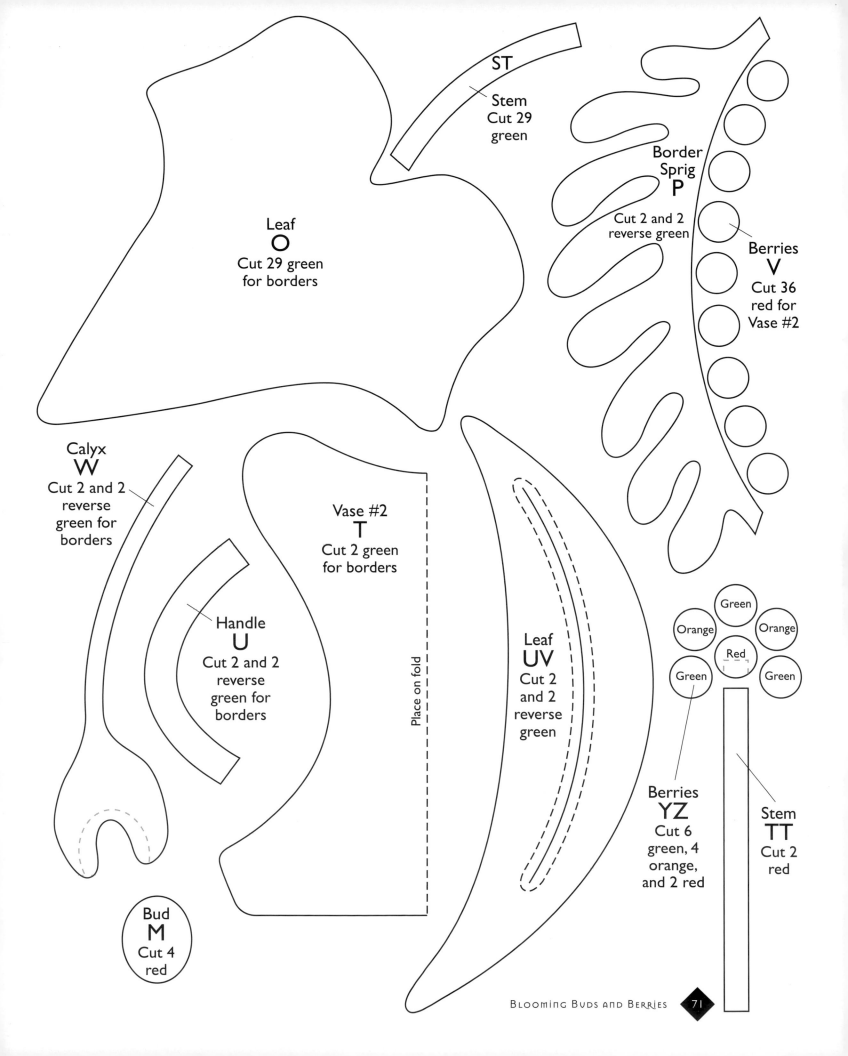

ST
Stem
Cut 29
green

Border
Sprig
P

Cut 2 and 2
reverse green

Berries
V
Cut 36
red for
Vase #2

Leaf
O
Cut 29 green
for borders

Calyx
W
Cut 2 and 2
reverse
green for
borders

Vase #2
T
Cut 2 green
for borders

Place on fold

Handle
U
Cut 2 and 2
reverse
green for
borders

Leaf
UV
Cut 2
and 2
reverse
green

Green
Orange
Orange
Red
Green
Green

Berries
YZ
Cut 6
green, 4
orange,
and 2 red

Stem
TT
Cut 2
red

Bud
M
Cut 4
red

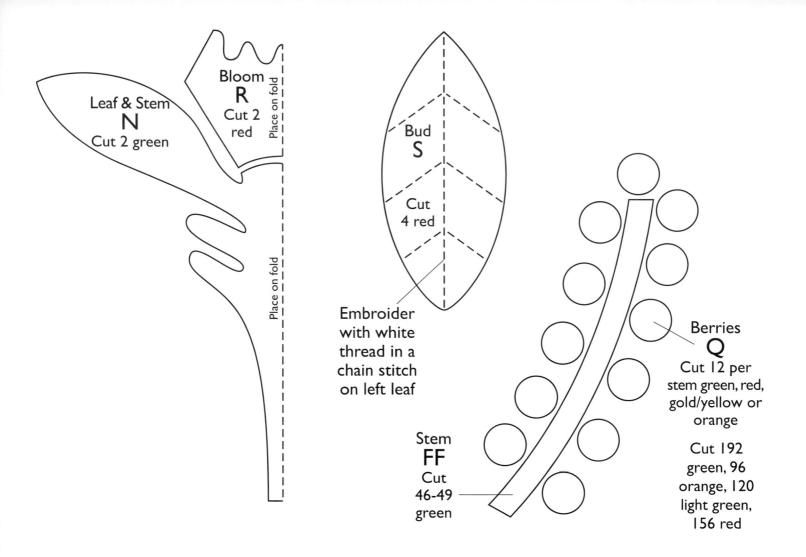

Leaf & Stem
N
Cut 2 green

Bloom
R
Cut 2 red

Place on fold

Place on fold

Bud
S

Cut
4 red

Embroider
with white
thread in a
chain stitch
on left leaf

Berries
Q

Cut 12 per
stem green, red,
gold/yellow or
orange

Cut 192
green, 96
orange, 120
light green,
156 red

Stem
FF
Cut
46-49
green

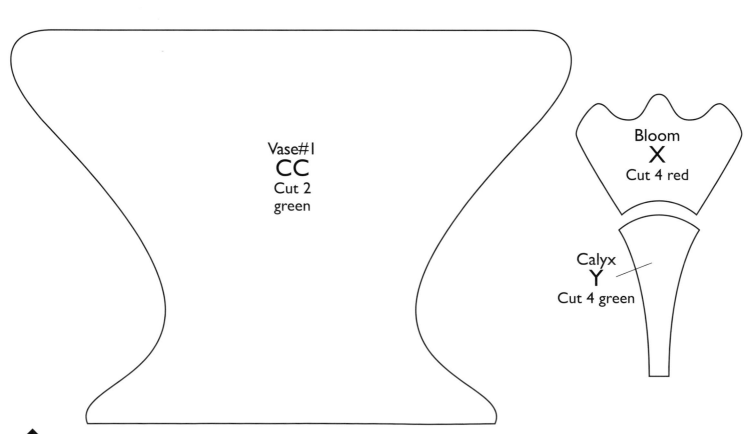

Vase#1
CC
Cut 2
green

Bloom
X
Cut 4 red

Calyx
Y
Cut 4 green

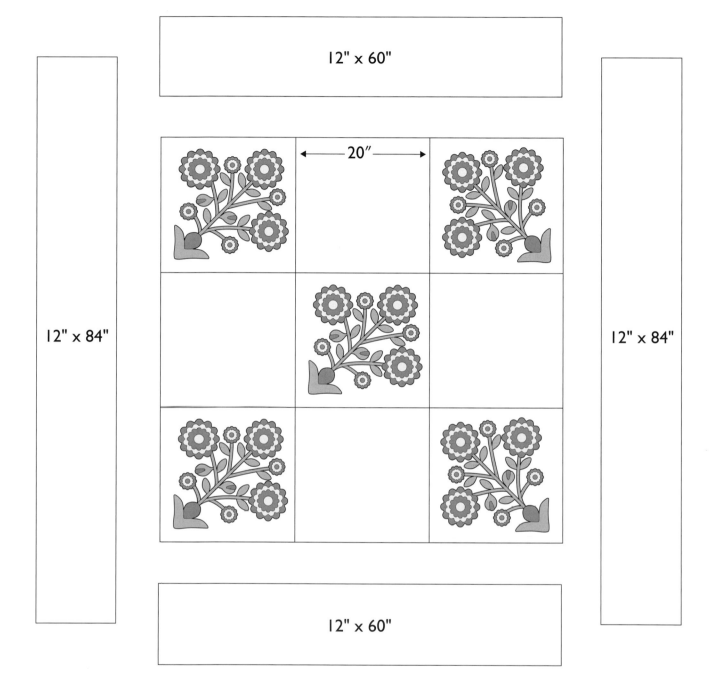

12" x 60"

12" x 84"

20"

12" x 84"

12" x 60"

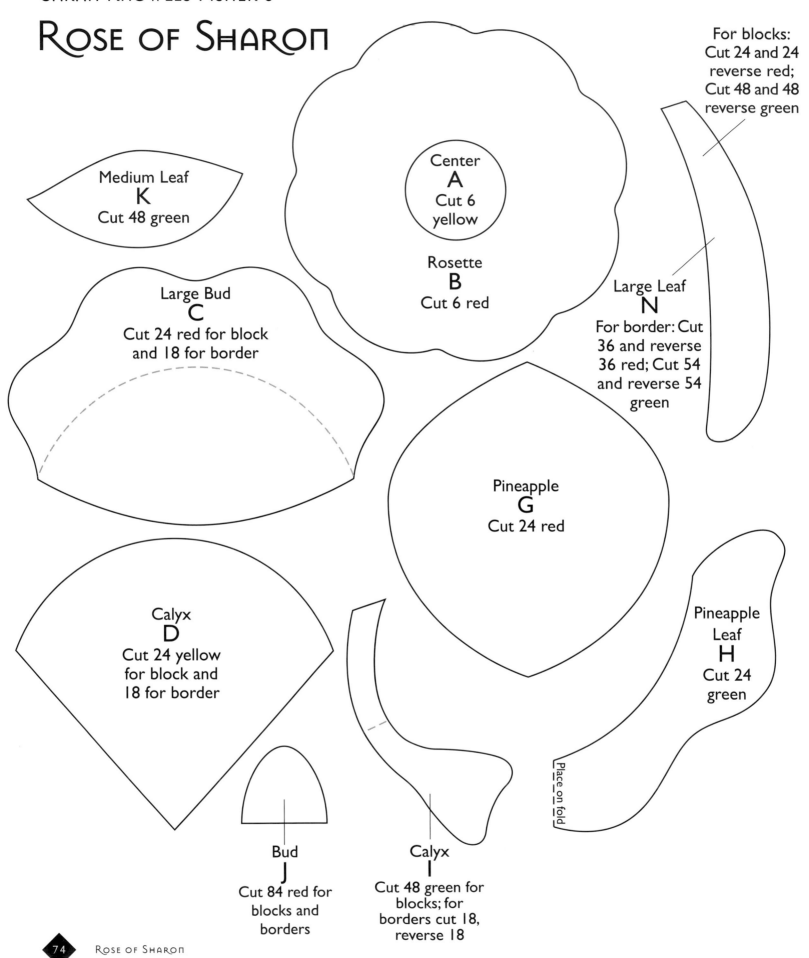

SARAH KNOWLES FISHER'S

ROSE OF SHARON

Medium Leaf
K
Cut 48 green

Center
A
Cut 6
yellow

Rosette
B
Cut 6 red

For blocks:
Cut 24 and 24
reverse red;
Cut 48 and 48
reverse green

Large Bud
C
Cut 24 red for block
and 18 for border

Large Leaf
N
For border: Cut
36 and reverse
36 red; Cut 54
and reverse 54
green

Pineapple
G
Cut 24 red

**Pineapple
Leaf**
H
Cut 24
green

Calyx
D
Cut 24 yellow
for block and
18 for border

Place on fold

Bud
J
Cut 84 red for
blocks and
borders

Calyx
I
Cut 48 green for
blocks; for
borders cut 18,
reverse 18

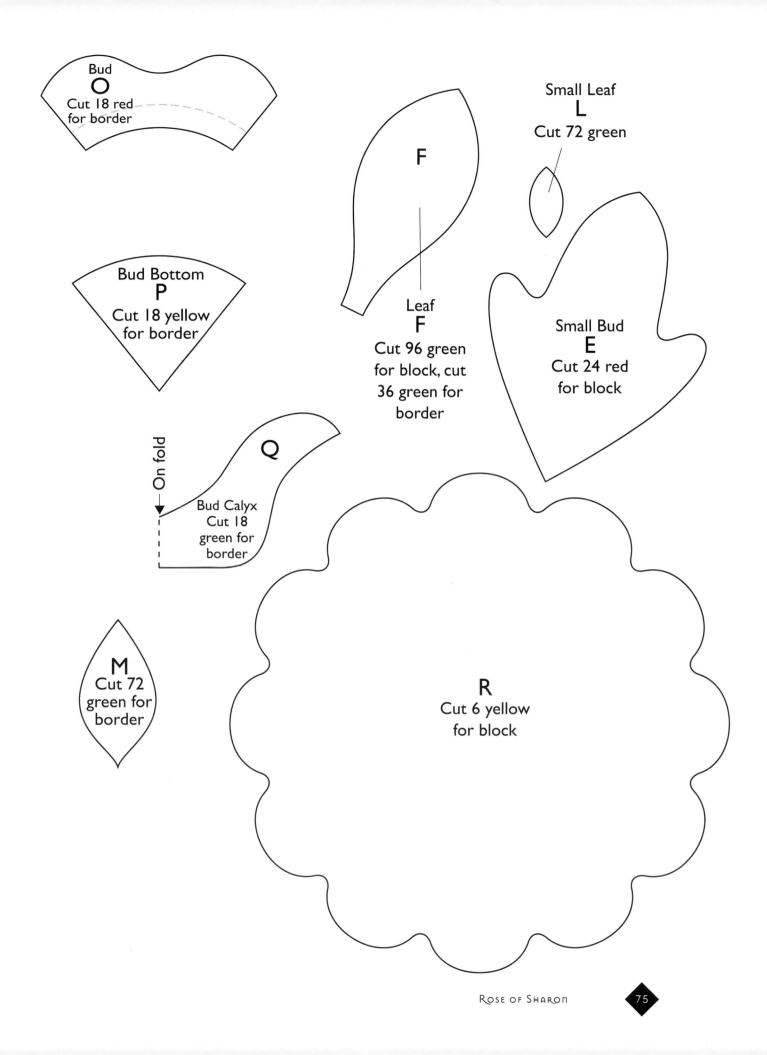

Bud
O
Cut 18 red
for border

Small Leaf
L
Cut 72 green

F

Bud Bottom
P
Cut 18 yellow
for border

Leaf
F
Cut 96 green
for block, cut
36 green for
border

Small Bud
E
Cut 24 red
for block

On fold

Q

Bud Calyx
Cut 18
green for
border

M
Cut 72
green for
border

R
Cut 6 yellow
for block

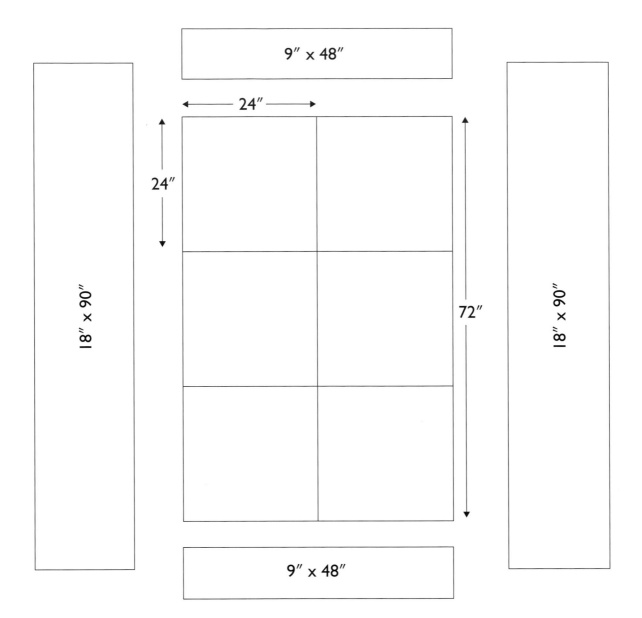

9" x 48"

24"

24"

18" x 90"

72"

18" x 90"

9" x 48"

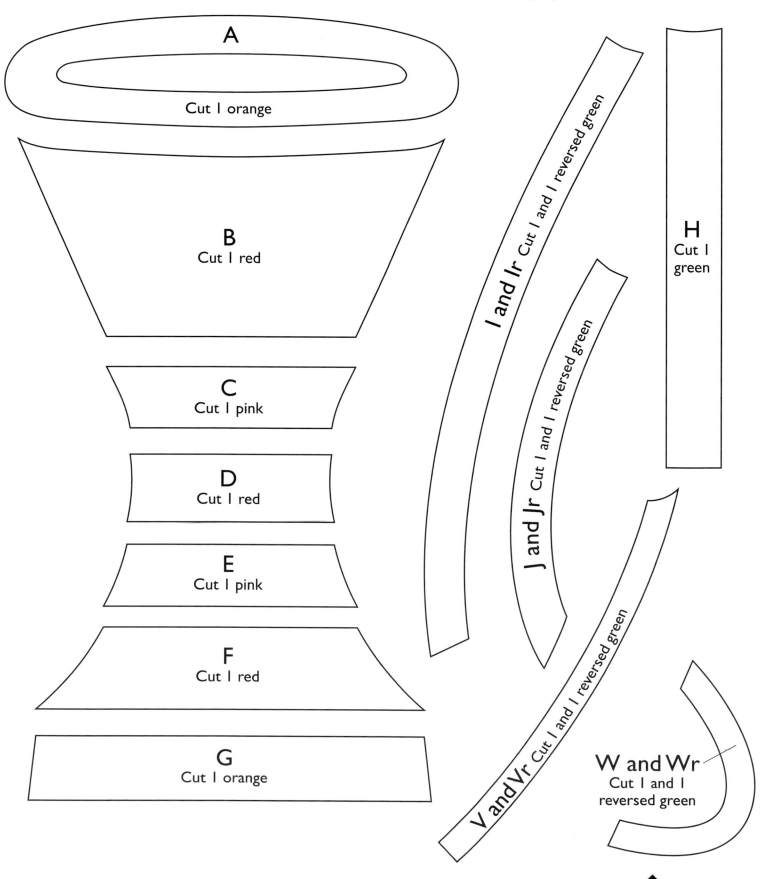

MARY PARKS LAWRENCE'S

CHERRY BASKETS

A
Cut 1 orange

B
Cut 1 red

C
Cut 1 pink

D
Cut 1 red

E
Cut 1 pink

F
Cut 1 red

G
Cut 1 orange

I and Ir Cut 1 and 1 reversed green

J and Jr Cut 1 and 1 reversed green

H
Cut 1
green

V and Vr Cut 1 and 1 reversed green

W and Wr
Cut 1 and 1
reversed green

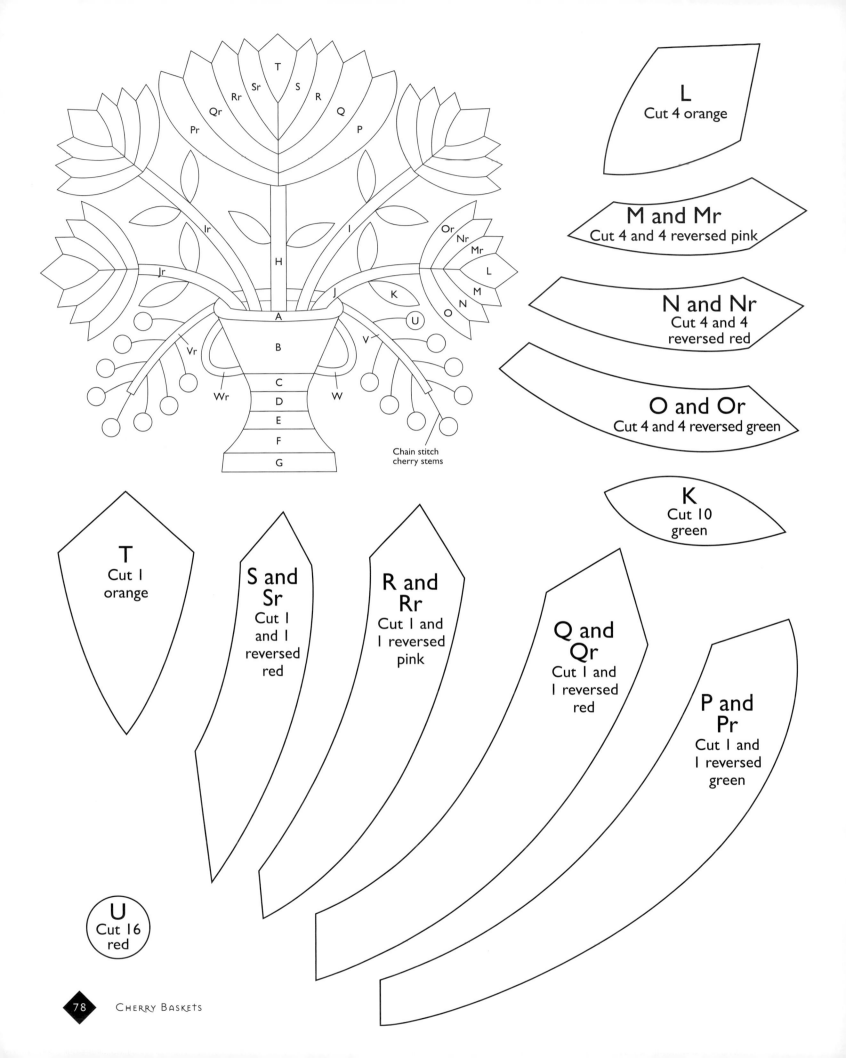

L
Cut 4 orange

M and Mr
Cut 4 and 4 reversed pink

N and Nr
Cut 4 and 4
reversed red

O and Or
Cut 4 and 4 reversed green

K
Cut 10
green

T
Cut 1
orange

S and
Sr
Cut 1
and 1
reversed
red

R and
Rr
Cut 1 and
1 reversed
pink

Q and
Qr
Cut 1 and
1 reversed
red

P and
Pr
Cut 1 and
1 reversed
green

U
Cut 16
red

Chain stitch
cherry stems

3" x 77"

← 11" → ← 22" →

3" x 72"

3" x 72"

3" x 77"

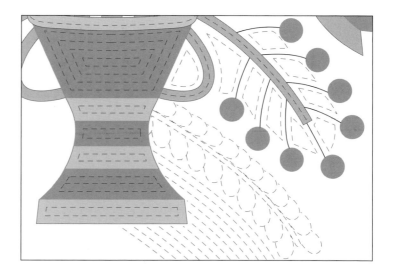

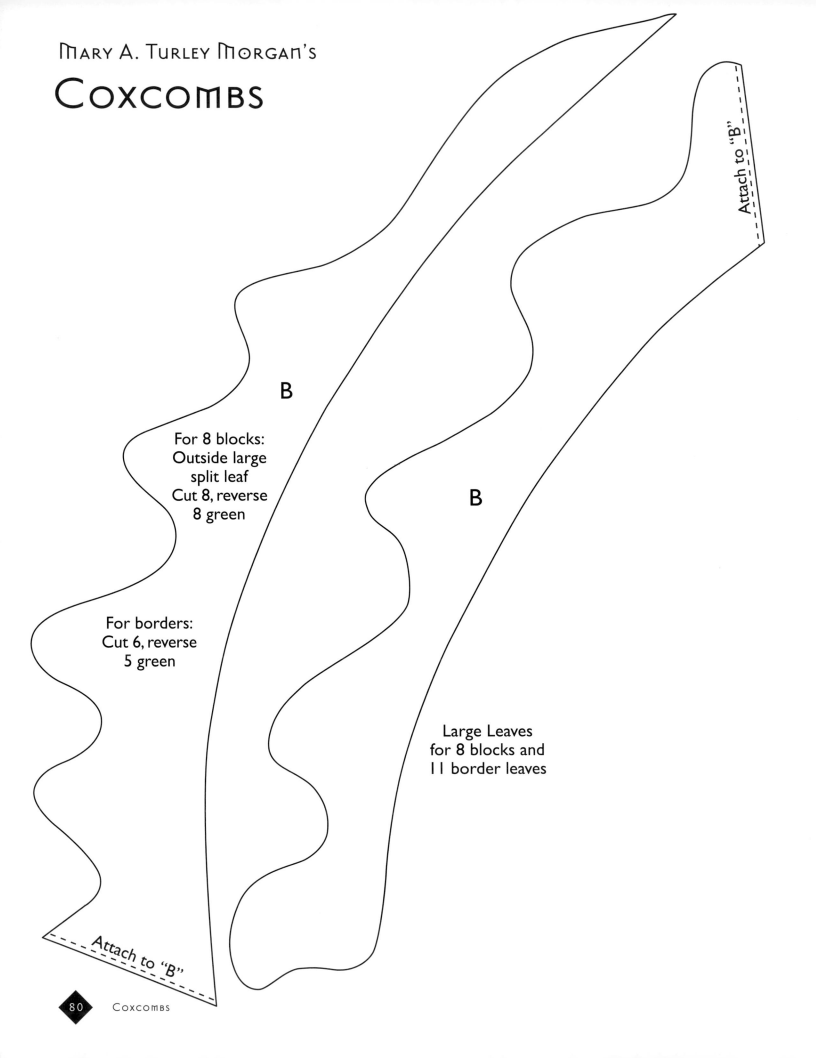

Mary A. Turley Morgan's

Coxcombs

B

For 8 blocks:
Outside large
split leaf
Cut 8, reverse
8 green

For borders:
Cut 6, reverse
5 green

B

Large Leaves
for 8 blocks and
11 border leaves

Attach to "B"

Attach to "B"

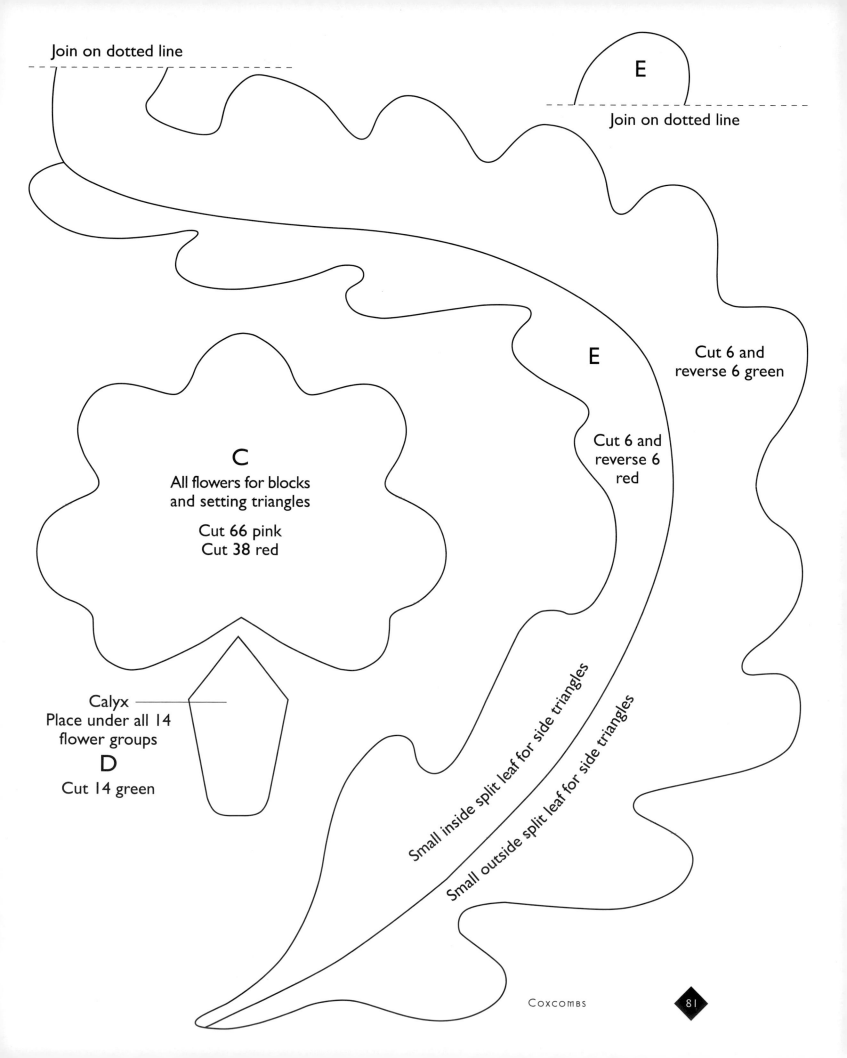

Join on dotted line

E

Join on dotted line

E

Cut 6 and
reverse 6 green

Cut 6 and
reverse 6
red

C

All flowers for blocks
and setting triangles

Cut 66 pink
Cut 38 red

Calyx
Place under all 14
flower groups

D

Cut 14 green

Small inside split leaf for side triangles

Small outside split leaf for side triangles

Rose Bud
F
Cut 14 red
for blocks
and setting
triangles

Calyx and Stem
G
Cut 14 green

H
Cut 4
green

J
Cut 4
pink

I
Cut 4 red

Applique 3 Sun
Wheels in the
corner triangles

K
Leaf
Cut 20
green

Add 18"
to end of
stem for 8
blocks

L
Cut 14
red

For ends of Long
Bud stems and,
joining leaves in the
6 side traingles

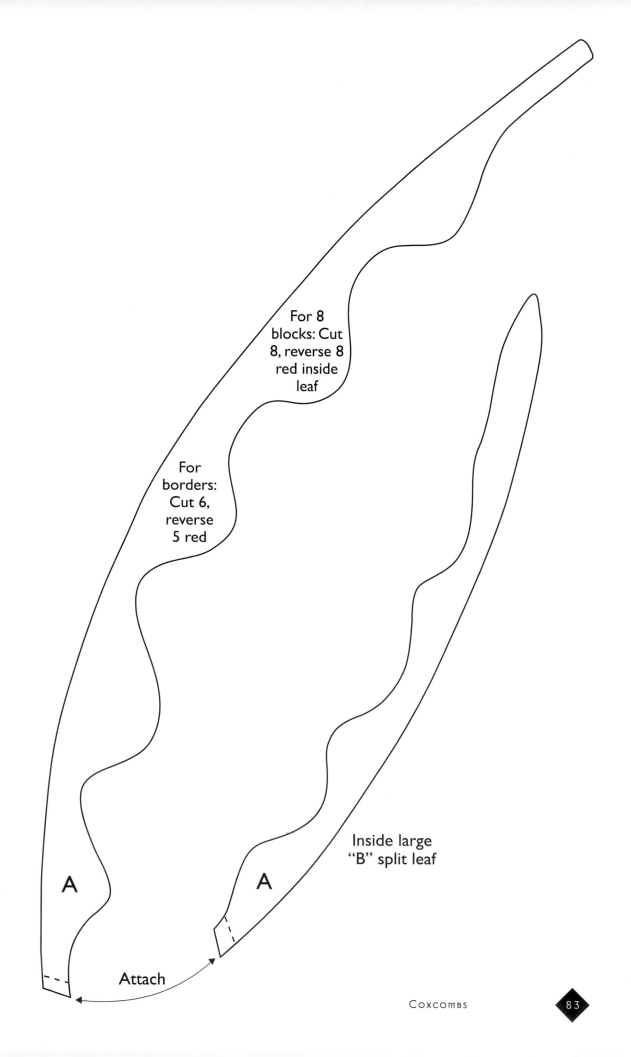

For 8 blocks: Cut 8, reverse 8 red inside leaf

For borders: Cut 6, reverse 5 red

Inside large "B" split leaf

A

A

Attach

Fig. #1

For six side setting
triangles, cut two 29 1/2"
squares. Cut on the
diagonal.

Fig. #2

For 4 corner triangles,
cut two 15"
squares. Cut on the
diagonal.

Fig. #3   No top border

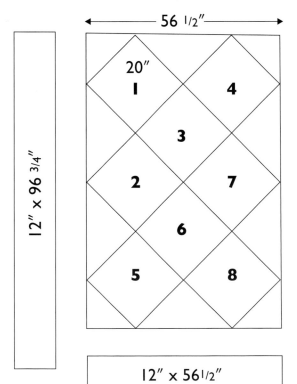

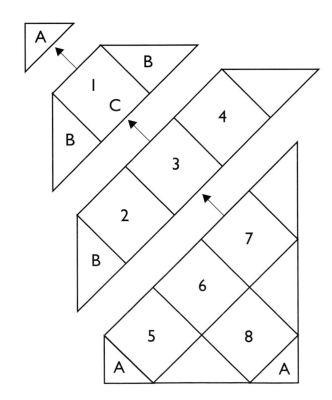

Happy Berries

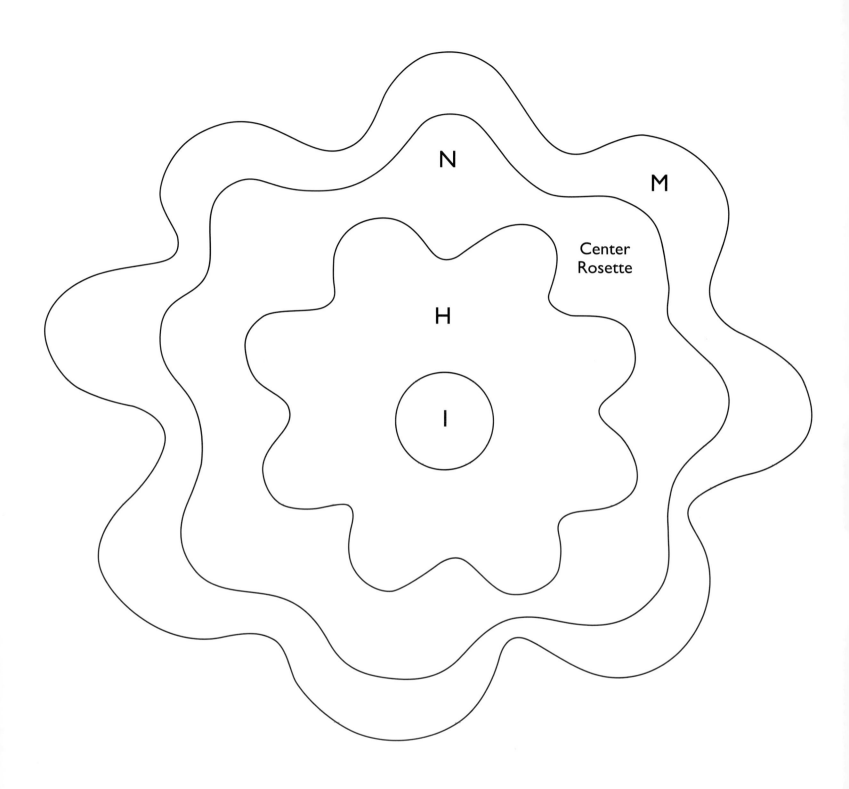

N

M

Center
Rosette

H

I

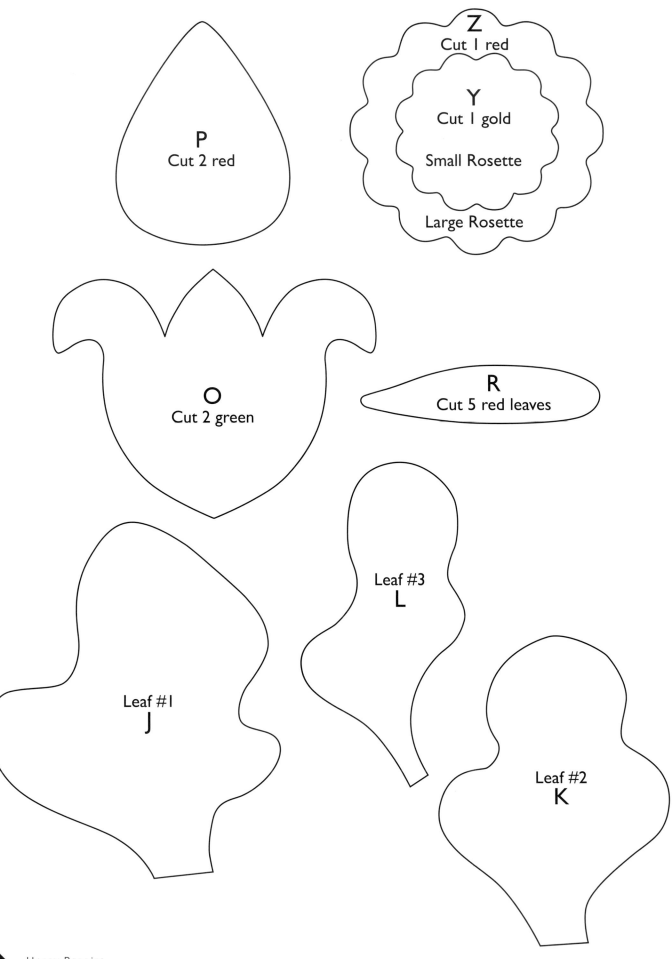

P
Cut 2 red

Z
Cut 1 red

Y
Cut 1 gold

Small Rosette

Large Rosette

O
Cut 2 green

R
Cut 5 red leaves

Leaf #3
L

Leaf #1
J

Leaf #2
K

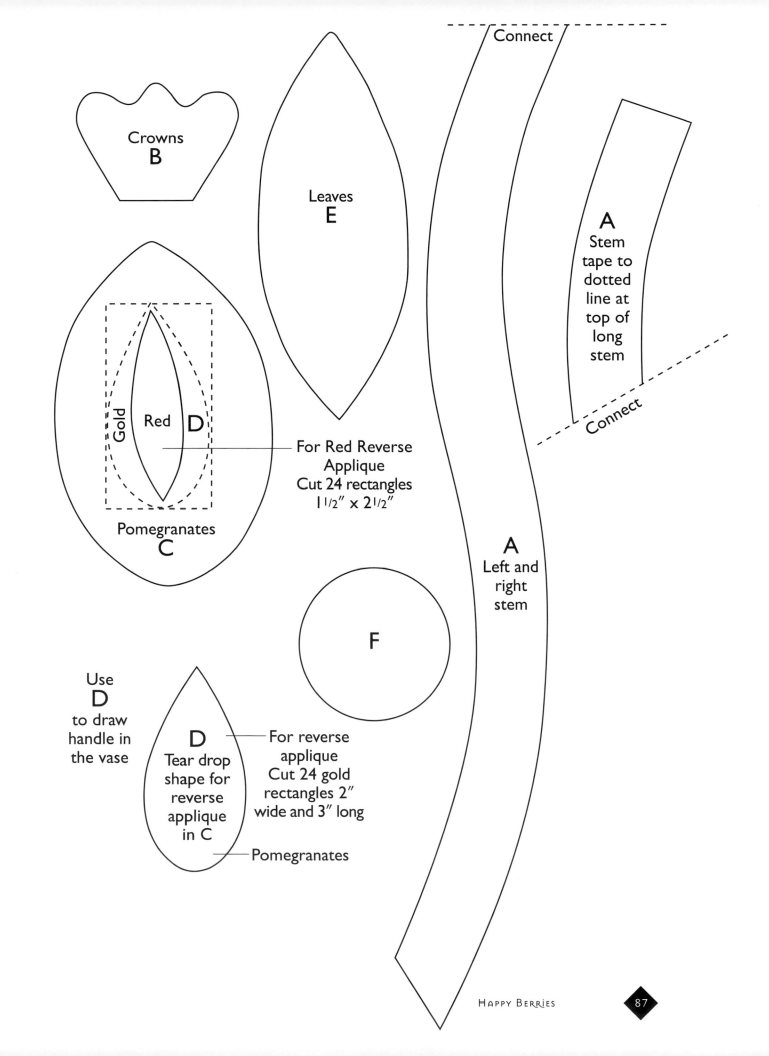

Crowns
B

Leaves
E

A
Stem tape to dotted line at top of long stem

Gold   Red   D

For Red Reverse Applique
Cut 24 rectangles
1 1/2" x 2 1/2"

Pomegranates
C

A
Left and right stem

F

Use
D
to draw handle in the vase

D
Tear drop shape for reverse applique in C

For reverse applique
Cut 24 gold rectangles 2" wide and 3" long

Pomegranates

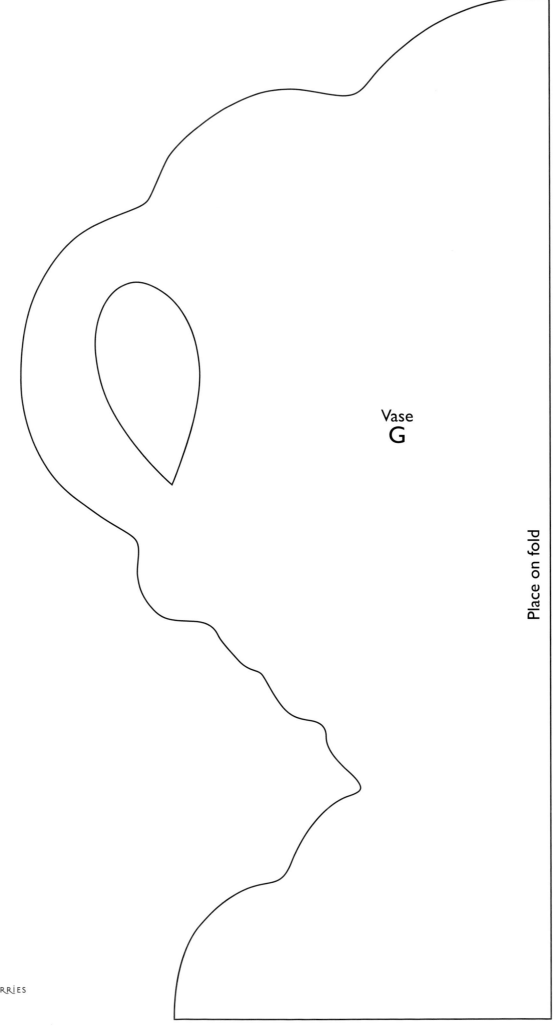

Vase
G

Place on fold

Terry's Berries

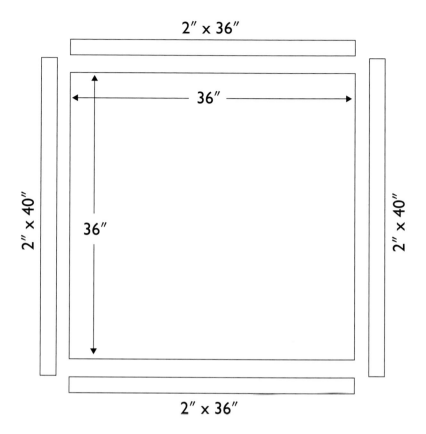

2″ x 36″

2″ x 40″

36″

36″

2″ x 40″

2″ x 36″

Nancy's Berries

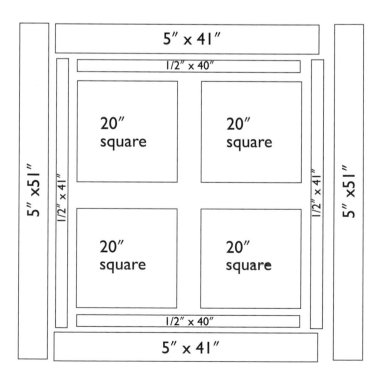

5″ x 41″

1/2″ x 40″

5″ x51″

1/2″ x 41″

20″ square

20″ square

1/2″ x 41″

5″ x51″

20″ square

20″ square

1/2″ x 40″

5″ x 41″

Unknown Maker

Indigo Feathers and Coxcombs

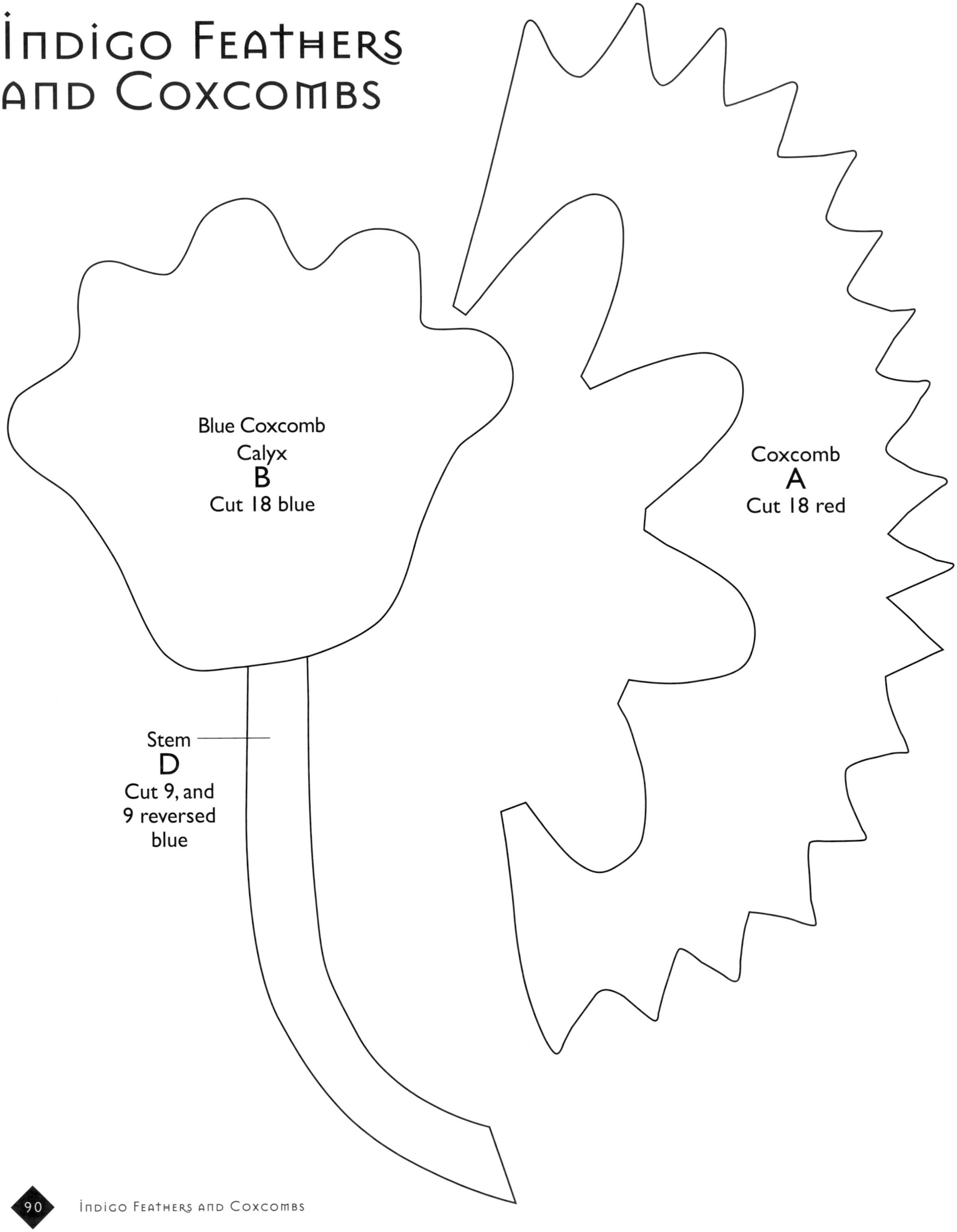
Blue Coxcomb
Calyx
B
Cut 18 blue
Coxcomb
A
Cut 18 red
Stem
D
Cut 9, and
9 reversed
blue

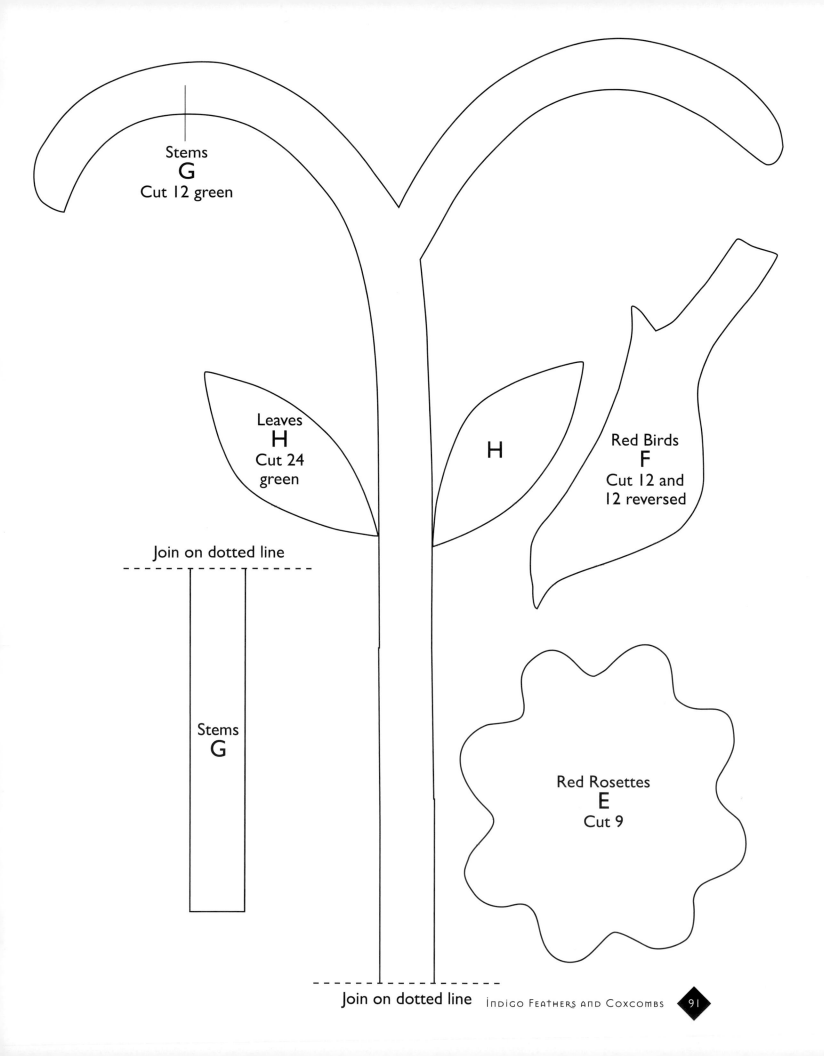

Stems
G
Cut 12 green

Leaves
H
Cut 24
green

H

Red Birds
F
Cut 12 and
12 reversed

Join on dotted line

Stems
G

Red Rosettes
E
Cut 9

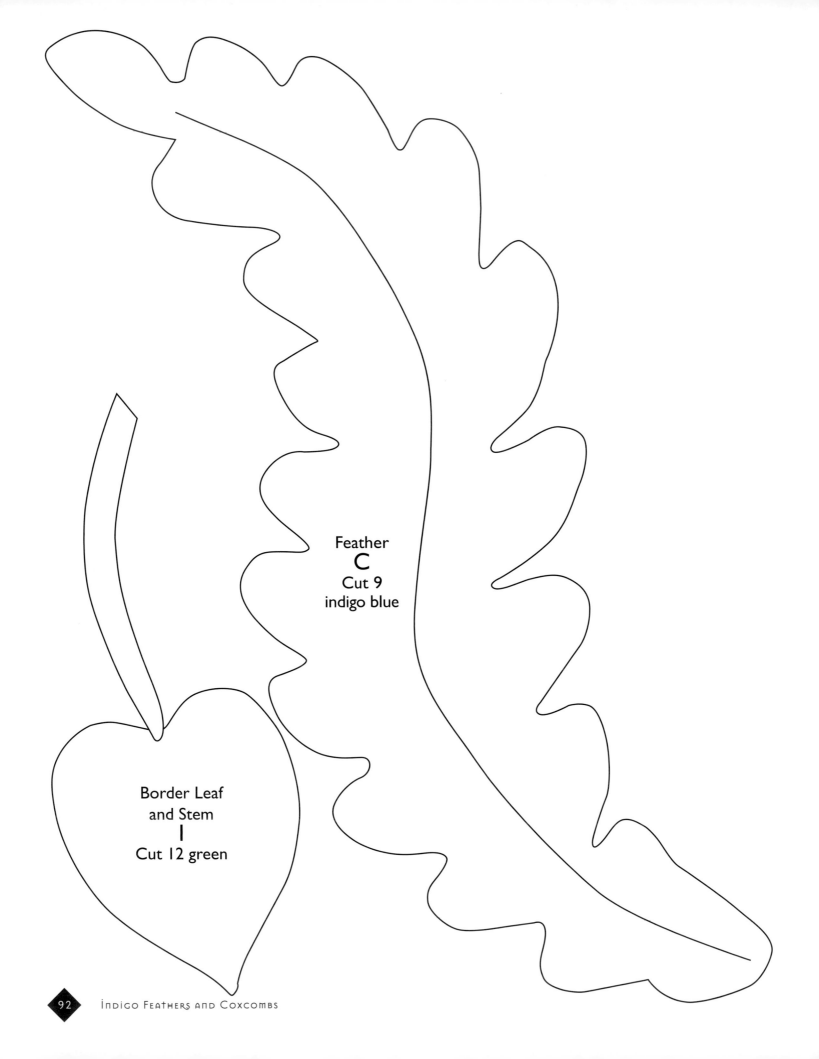

Feather
C
Cut 9
indigo blue

Border Leaf
and Stem
I
Cut 12 green

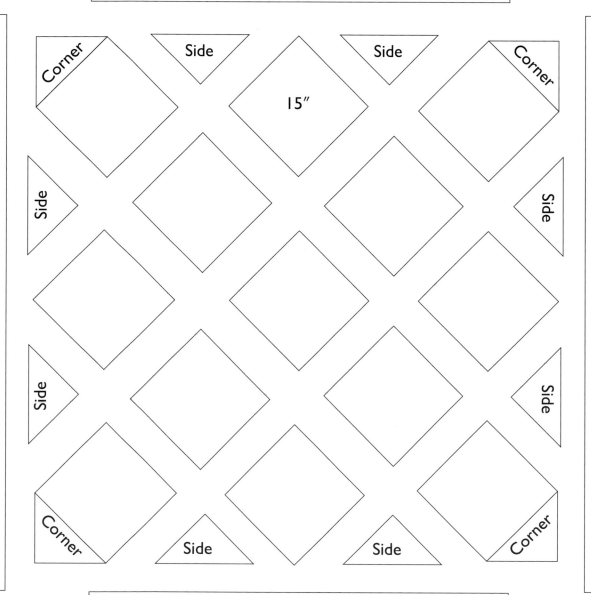

12″ x 63 3/4″

12″ x 87 3/4″

12″ x 87 3/4″

Corner

Side

Side

Corner

15″

Side

Side

Side

Side

Corner

Side

Side

Corner

12″ x 63 3/4″

OLD MEXICAN ROSE

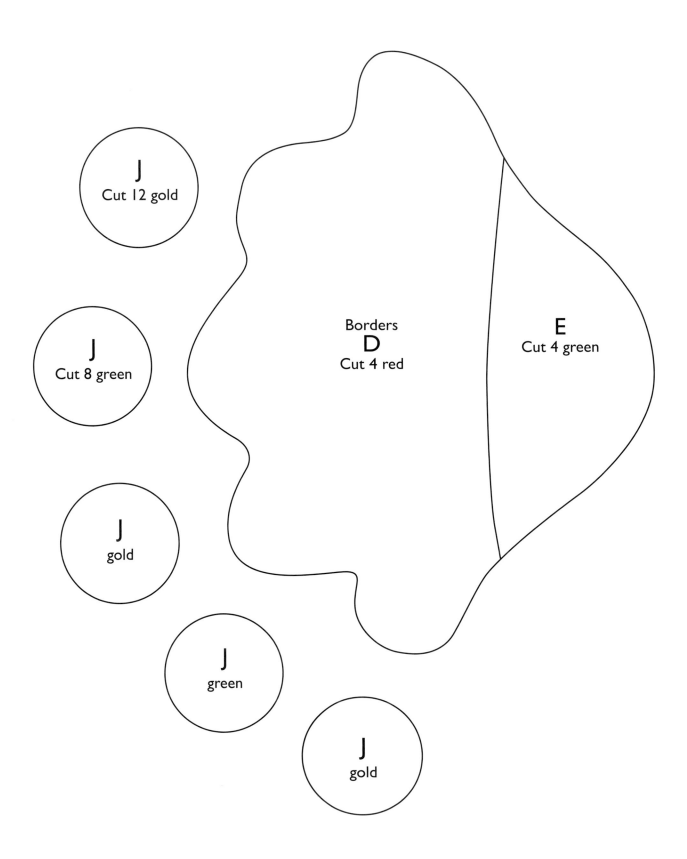

J
Cut 12 gold

J
Cut 8 green

J
gold

J
green

J
gold

Borders
D
Cut 4 red

E
Cut 4 green

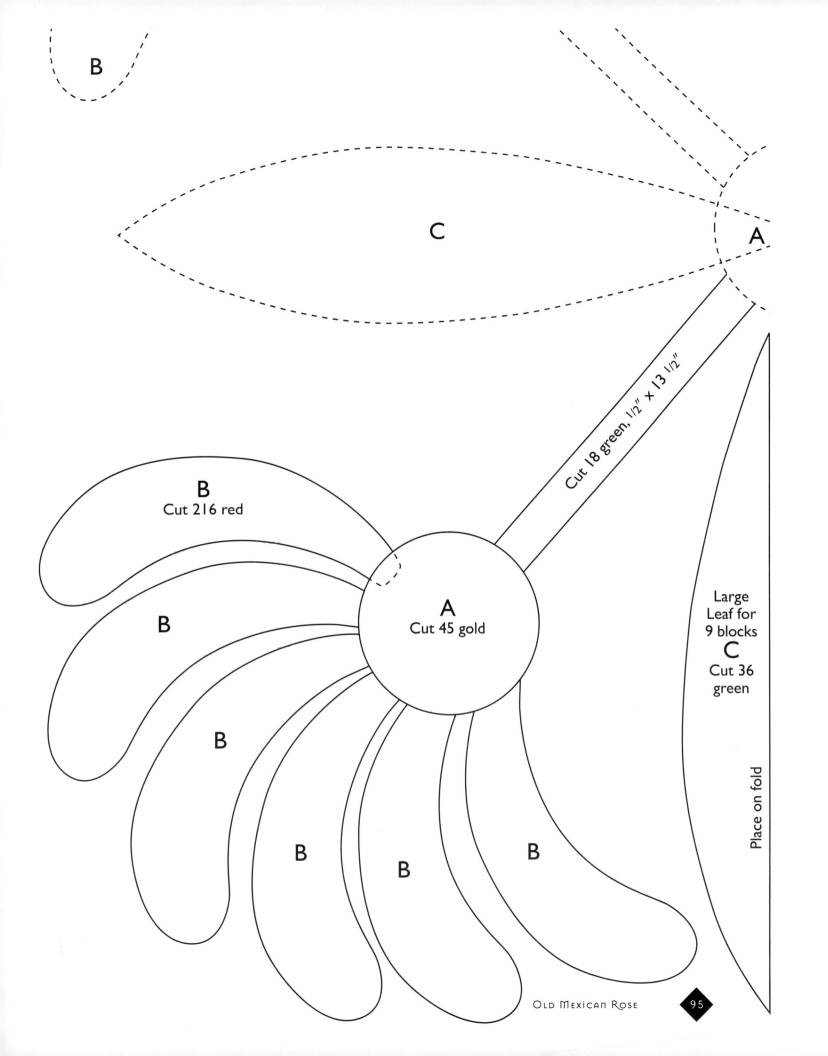

B

C

A

B
Cut 216 red

Cut 18 green, 1/2" x 13 1/2"

B

B

A
Cut 45 gold

Large
Leaf for
9 blocks
C
Cut 36
green

B

B

B

B

Place on fold

Old Mexican Rose

95

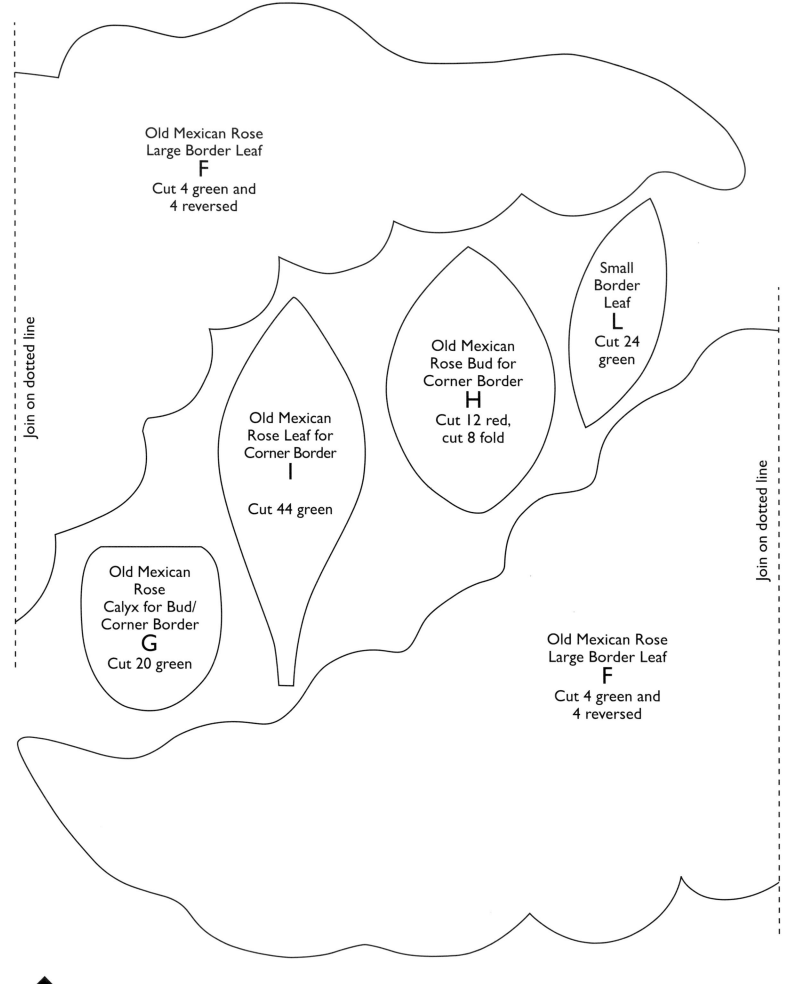

Old Mexican Rose
Large Border Leaf
F

Cut 4 green and
4 reversed

Small
Border
Leaf
L
Cut 24
green

Old Mexican
Rose Bud for
Corner Border
H

Cut 12 red,
cut 8 fold

Old Mexican
Rose Leaf for
Corner Border
I

Cut 44 green

Old Mexican
Rose
Calyx for Bud/
Corner Border
G
Cut 20 green

Old Mexican Rose
Large Border Leaf
F

Cut 4 green and
4 reversed

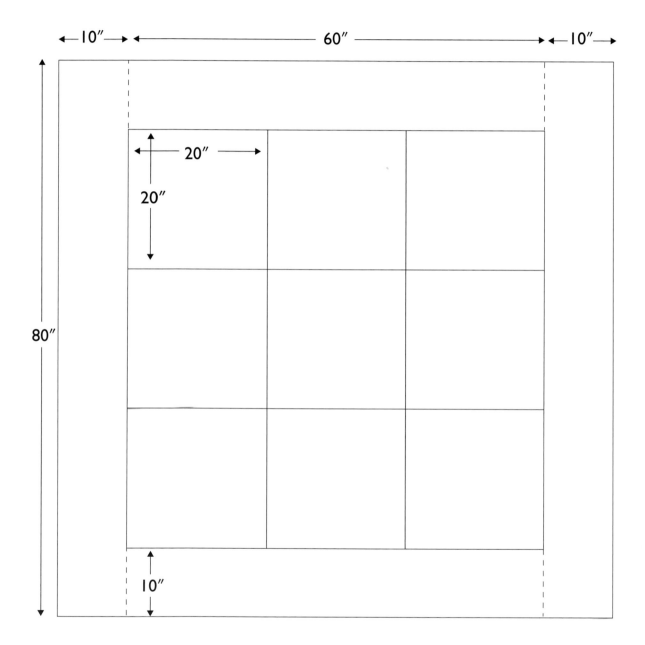

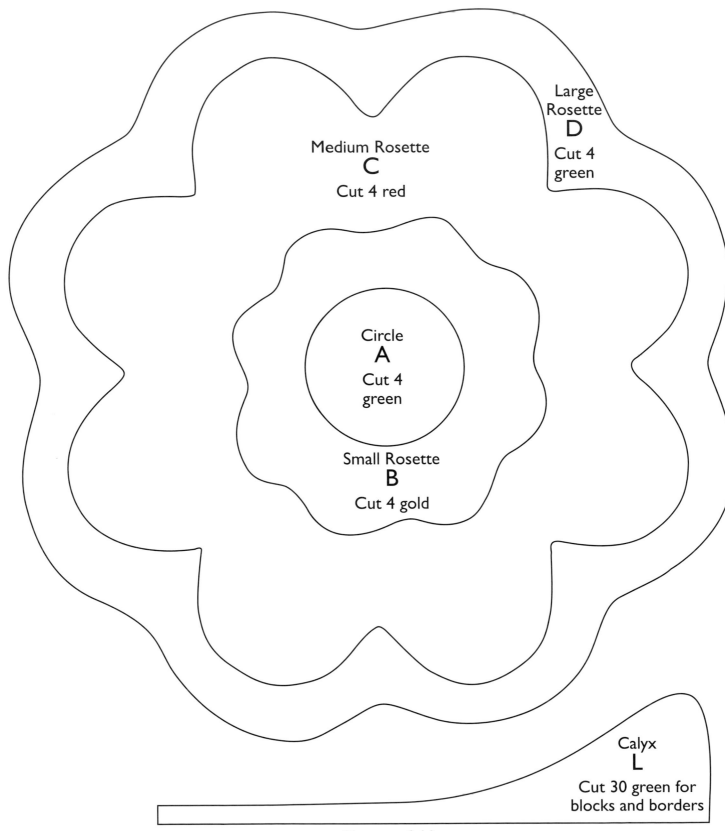

Christmas Cactus

Large
Rosette
D
Cut 4
green

Medium Rosette
C
Cut 4 red

Circle
A
Cut 4
green

Small Rosette
B
Cut 4 gold

Calyx
L
Cut 30 green for
blocks and borders

Place on fold

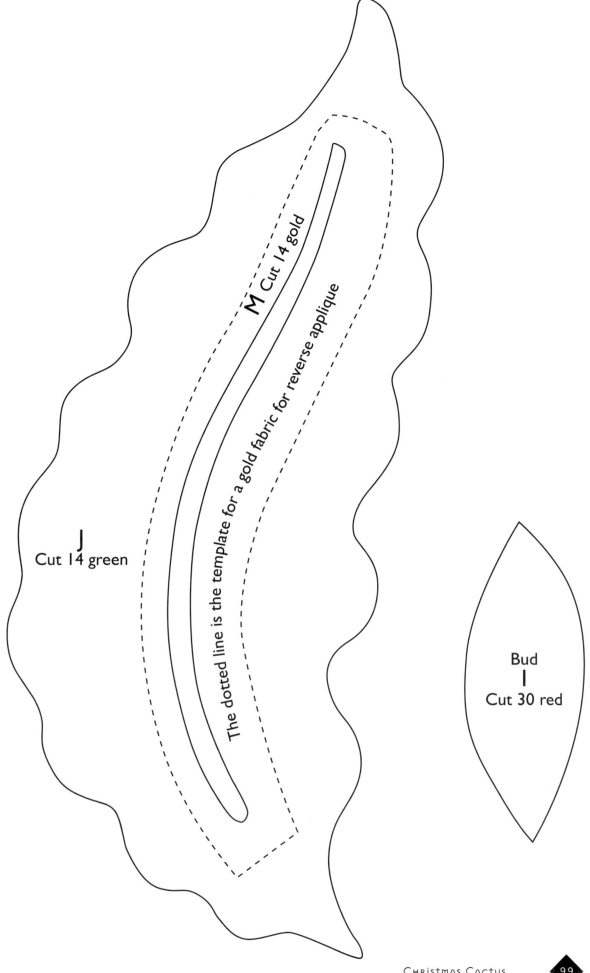

M Cut 14 gold

J
Cut 14 green

The dotted line is the template for a gold fabric for reverse applique

Bud
I
Cut 30 red

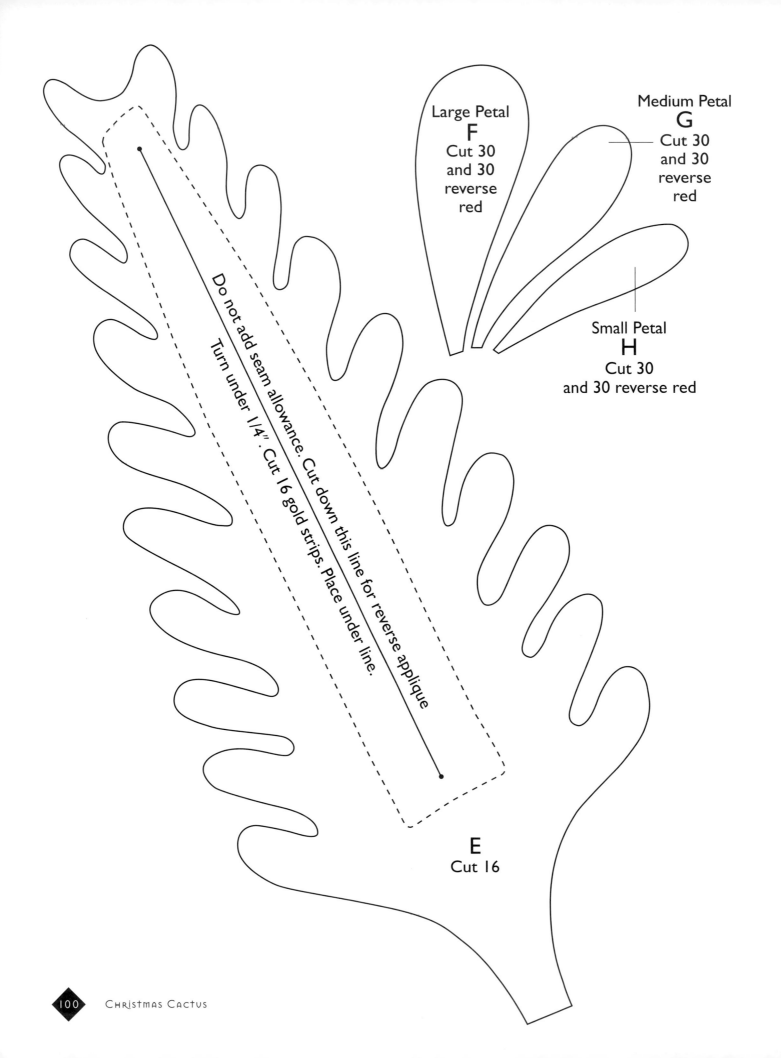

Large Petal
F
Cut 30
and 30
reverse
red

Medium Petal
G
Cut 30
and 30
reverse
red

Small Petal
H
Cut 30
and 30 reverse red

Do not add seam allowance. Cut down this line for reverse appliqué

Turn under 1/4". Cut 16 gold strips. Place under line.

E
Cut 16

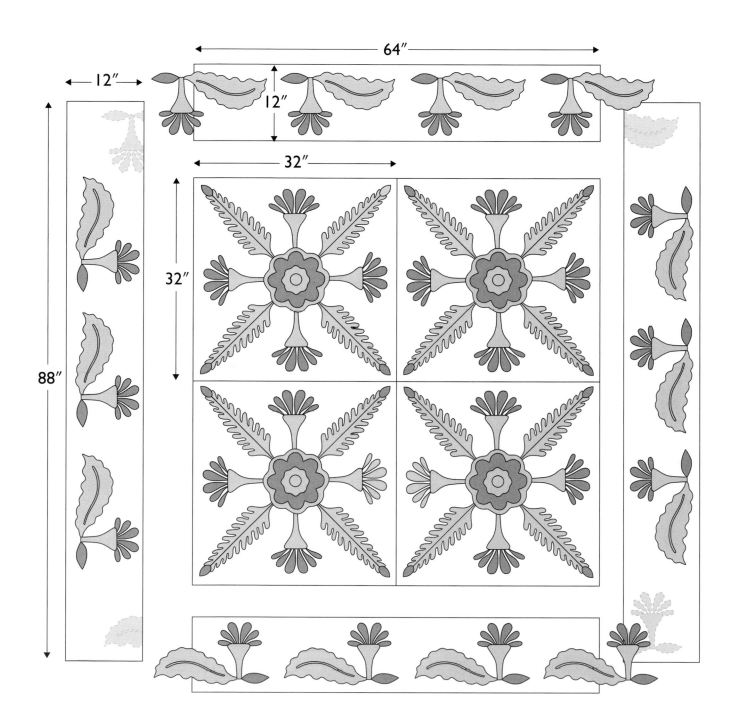

64"

12"

12"

32"

32"

88"

ROSE TREE

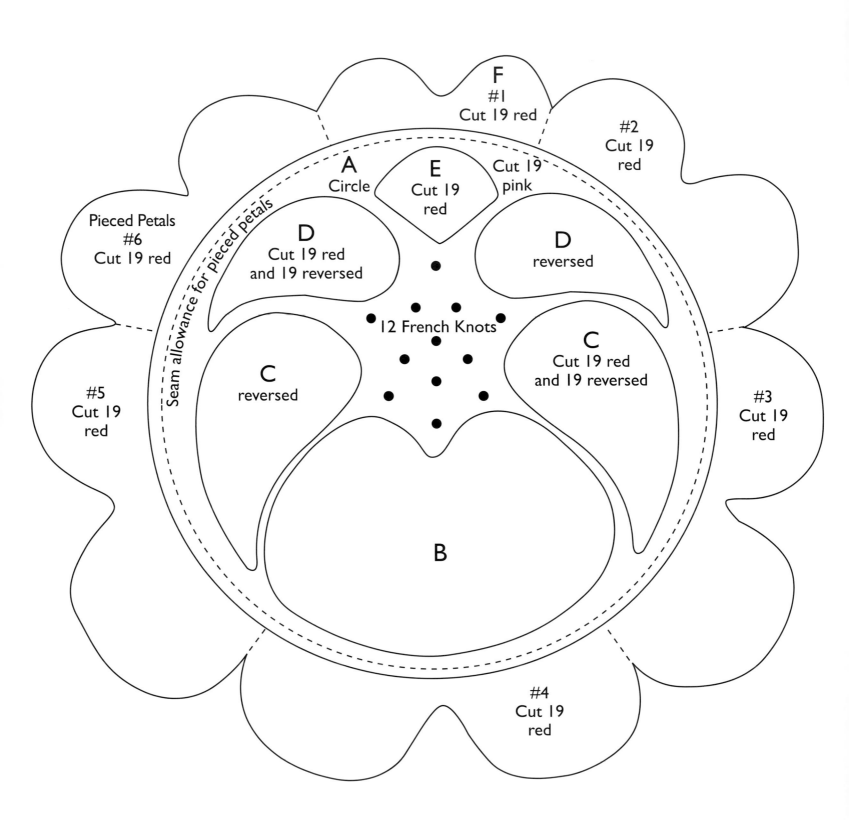

Pieced Petals
#6
Cut 19 red

Seam allowance for pieced petals

A
Circle

E
Cut 19
red

Cut 19
pink

F
#1
Cut 19 red

#2
Cut 19
red

D
Cut 19 red
and 19 reversed

D
reversed

12 French Knots

C
reversed

C
Cut 19 red
and 19 reversed

#5
Cut 19
red

#3
Cut 19
red

B

#4
Cut 19
red

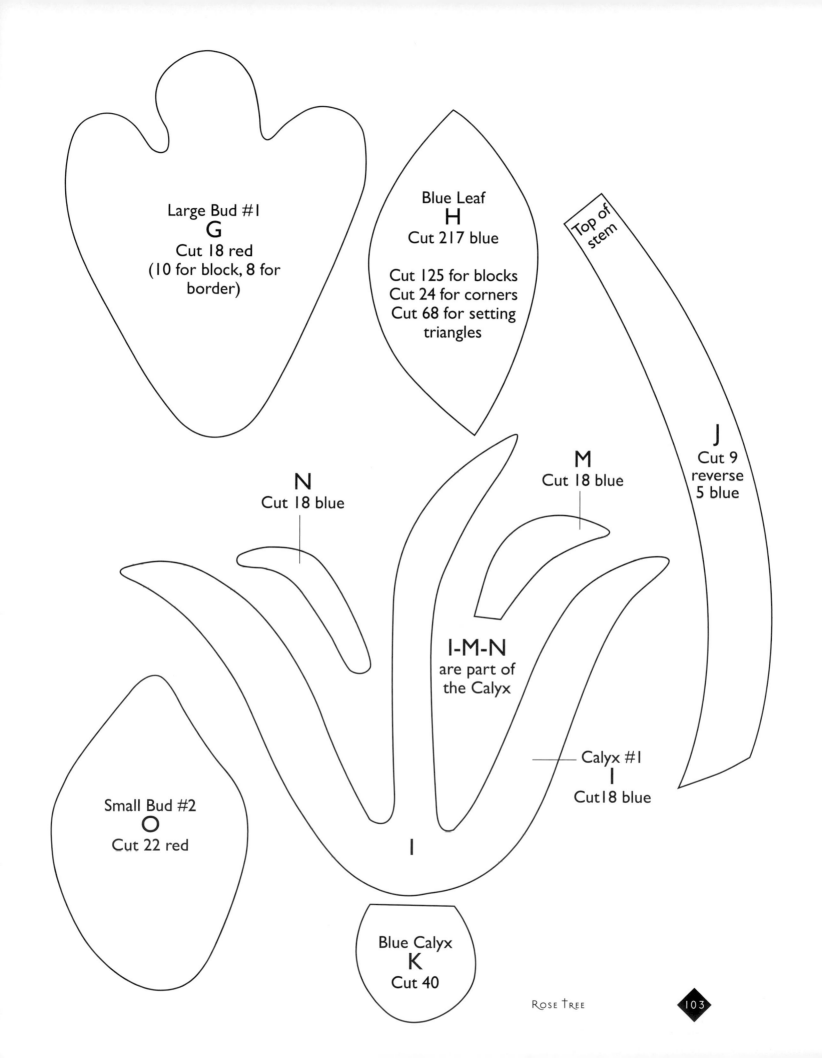

Large Bud #1
G
Cut 18 red
(10 for block, 8 for border)

Blue Leaf
H
Cut 217 blue

Cut 125 for blocks
Cut 24 for corners
Cut 68 for setting triangles

Top of stem

J
Cut 9 reverse
5 blue

N
Cut 18 blue

M
Cut 18 blue

I-M-N
are part of the Calyx

Calyx #1
I
Cut18 blue

I

Small Bud #2
O
Cut 22 red

Blue Calyx
K
Cut 40

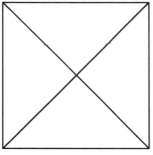

Fig. #1
Cut one 42¹/₄-inch
square for four
setting side triangles

Fig. #2
Cut two 21³/₈-inch
squares for four
corner triangles

Fig. #3

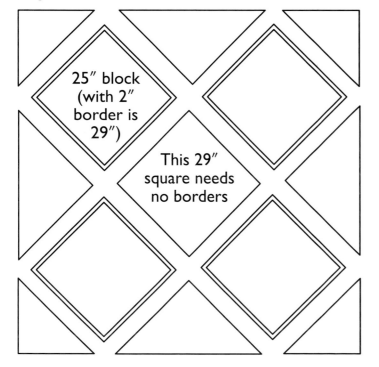

25" block
(with 2"
border is
29")

This 29"
square needs
no borders

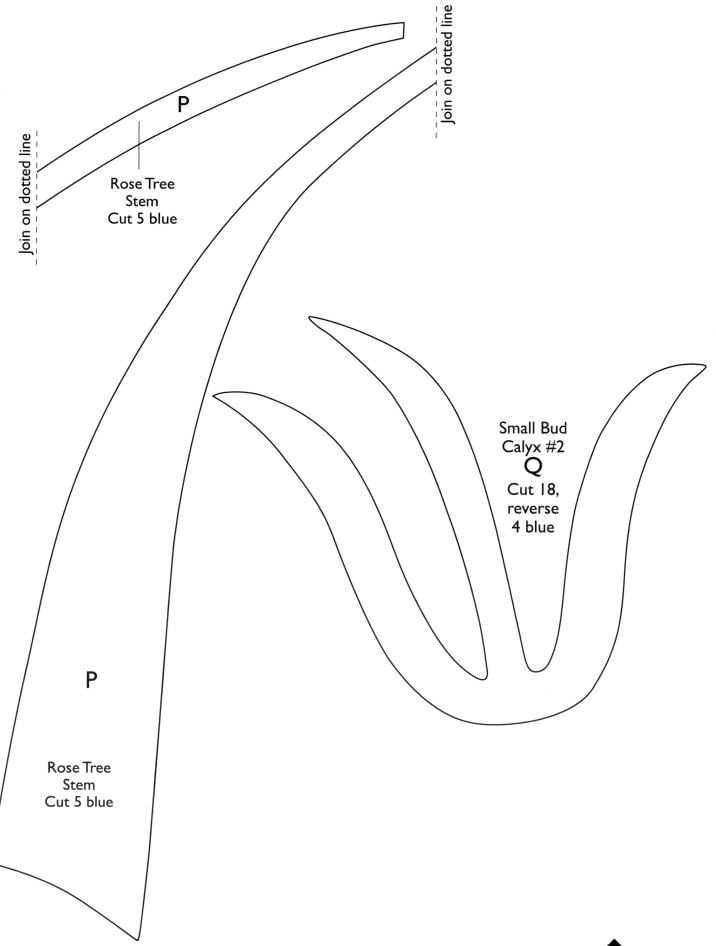

P

Rose Tree
Stem
Cut 5 blue

Small Bud
Calyx #2
Q
Cut 18,
reverse
4 blue

P

Rose Tree
Stem
Cut 5 blue

BASKET OF TULIPS

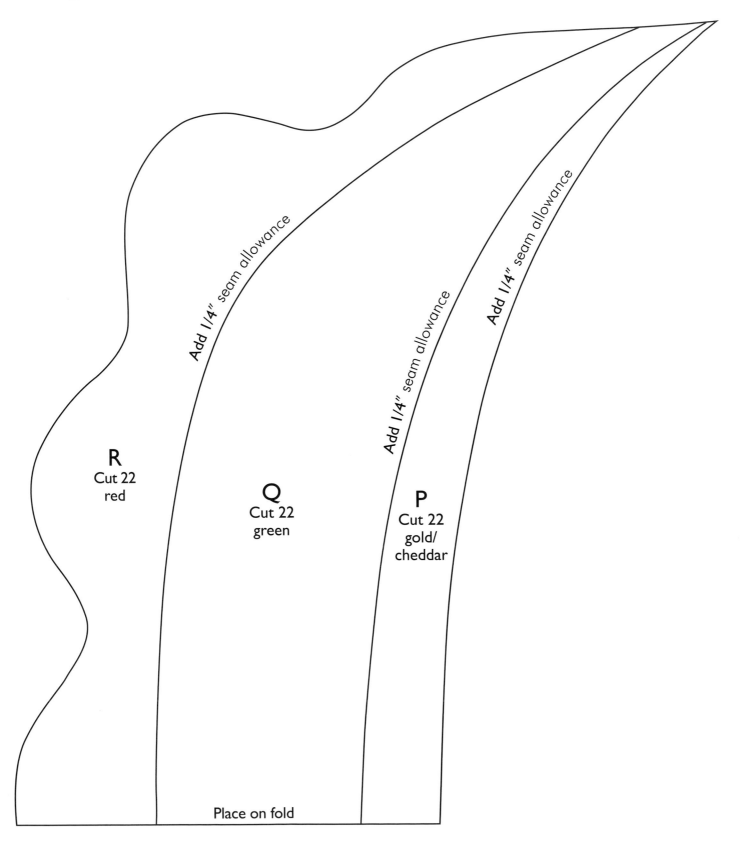

R
Cut 22
red

Q
Cut 22
green

P
Cut 22
gold/
cheddar

Add 1/4" seam allowance

Add 1/4" seam allowance

Add 1/4" seam allowance

Place on fold

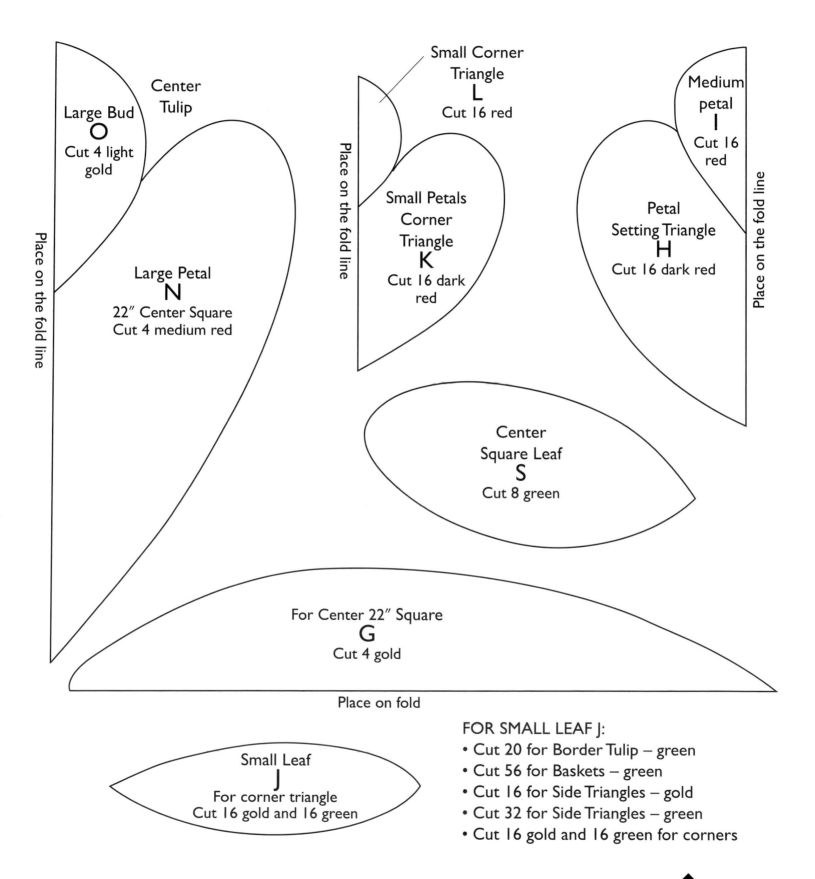

Small Corner
Triangle
L
Cut 16 red

Large Bud
O
Cut 4 light
gold

Center
Tulip

Medium
petal
I
Cut 16
red

Place on the fold line

Large Petal
N
22" Center Square
Cut 4 medium red

Small Petals
Corner
Triangle
K
Cut 16 dark
red

Petal
Setting Triangle
H
Cut 16 dark red

Place on the fold line

Place on the fold line

Center
Square Leaf
S
Cut 8 green

For Center 22" Square
G
Cut 4 gold

Place on fold

Small Leaf
J
For corner triangle
Cut 16 gold and 16 green

FOR SMALL LEAF J:
• Cut 20 for Border Tulip – green
• Cut 56 for Baskets – green
• Cut 16 for Side Triangles – gold
• Cut 32 for Side Triangles – green
• Cut 16 gold and 16 green for corners

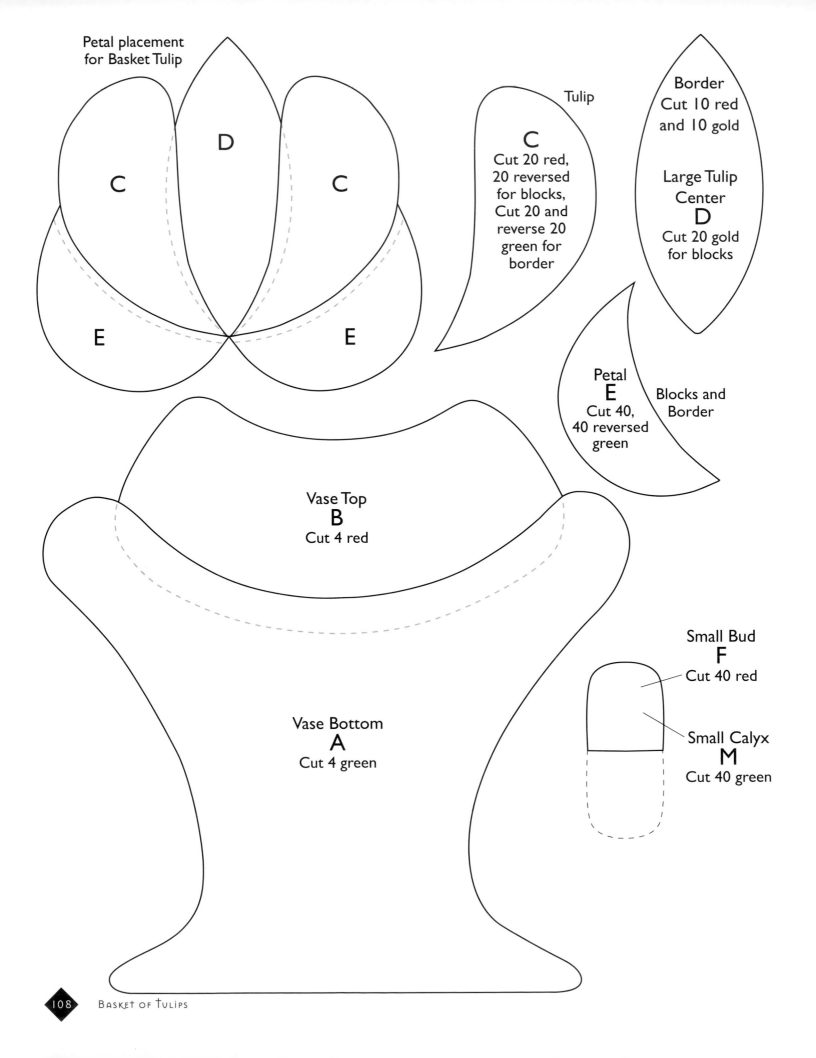

Petal placement
for Basket Tulip

C

D

C

E

E

Tulip

C

Cut 20 red,
20 reversed
for blocks,
Cut 20 and
reverse 20
green for
border

Border
Cut 10 red
and 10 gold

Large Tulip
Center
D
Cut 20 gold
for blocks

Petal
E
Cut 40,
40 reversed
green

Blocks and
Border

Vase Top
B
Cut 4 red

Small Bud
F
Cut 40 red

Small Calyx
M
Cut 40 green

Vase Bottom
A
Cut 4 green

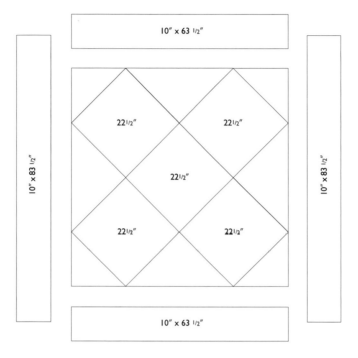

10″ x 63 ¹/₂″

10″ x 83 ¹/₂″

10″ x 83 ¹/₂″

22¹/₂″   22¹/₂″

22¹/₂″

22¹/₂″   22¹/₂″

10″ x 63 ¹/₂″

Quilting Designs

Stitch 1 (1 of 2)

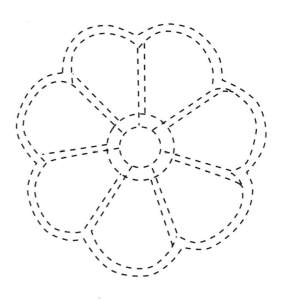

STİTCH I (2 OF 2)

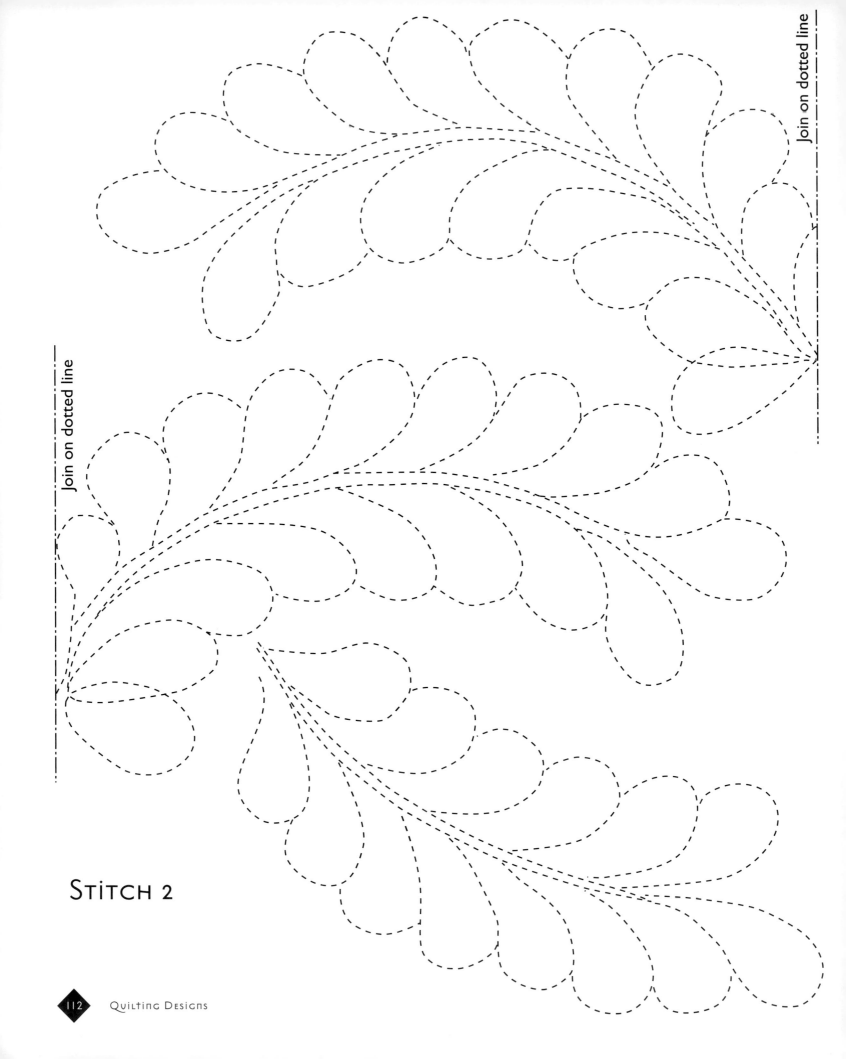

Join on dotted line

Join on dotted line

Join on dotted line

STITCH 2

Join on dotted line

STITCH 3

Join on dotted line

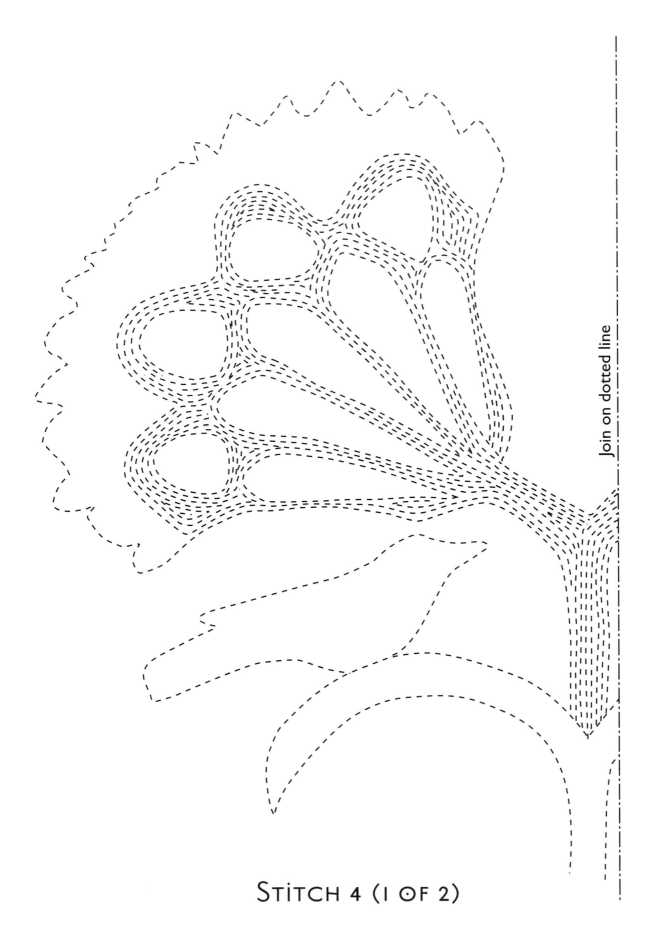

Join on dotted line

STITCH 4 (1 OF 2)

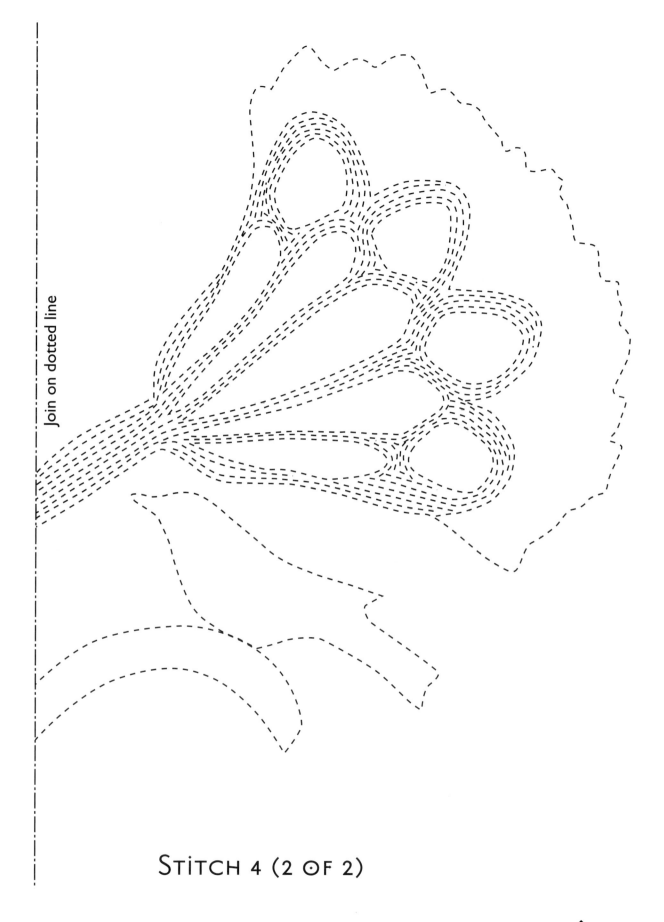

Join on dotted line

STITCH 4 (2 OF 2)

Join on dotted line

STITCH 5 (1 OF 2)

STITCH 5 (2 OF 2)

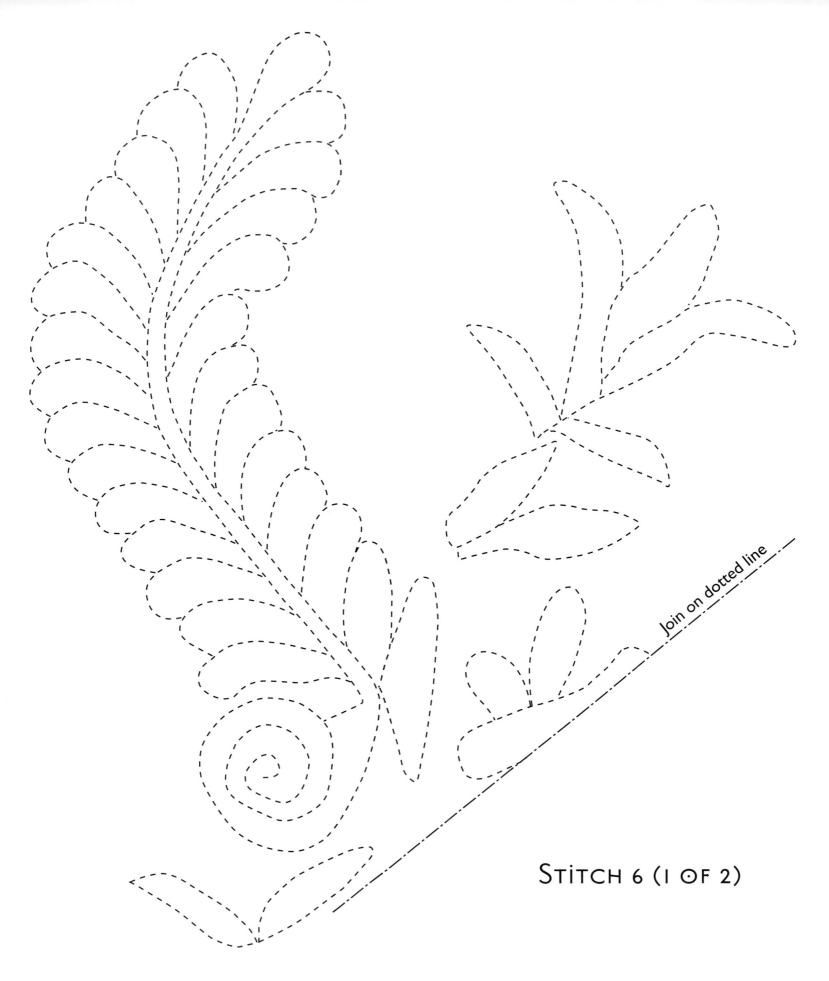

Join on dotted line

STITCH 6 (1 OF 2)

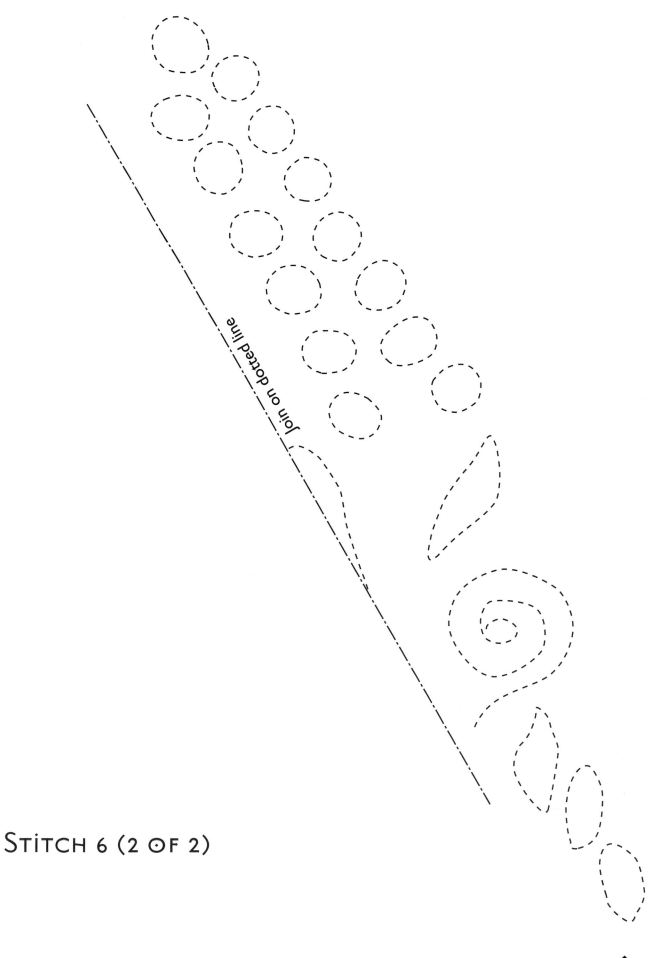

Join on dotted line

STITCH 6 (2 OF 2)

STITCH 7

Join on dotted line

Stitch 8 (1 of 2)

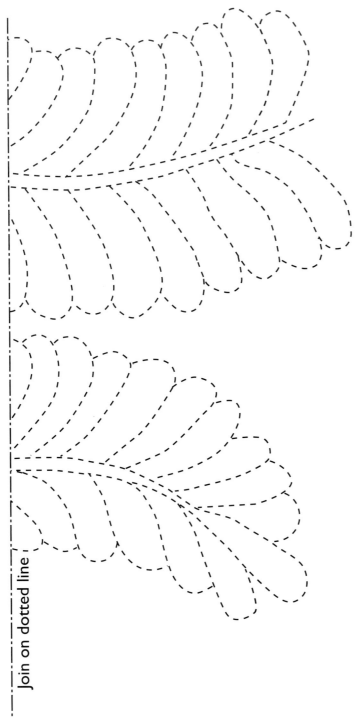

Join on dotted line

STITCH 8 (2 OF 2)

Suggested reading

Brackman, Barbara. *Encyclopedia of Appliqué*. McLean, Virginia: EPM Publications, Inc, 1993.

_____, "Emporia, 1935-1950: Reflections on a Community," in *Kansas Quilts and Quilters*. Lawrence, KS: University Press of Kansas, 1993.

Clark, Ricky. *Quilted Gardens: Floral Quilts of the Nineteenth Century*. Nashville, TN: Rutledge Hill Press, 1994.

Crews, Patricia Cox, ed., *A Flowering of Quilts*. Lincoln, NE: University of Nebraska Press, 2001.

Ewer, Helen, "Four Block Quilts," in *Blanket Statements*, Lincoln, NE: Newsletter of the American Quilt Study Group, Fall 2005.

Hornback, Nancy, "Nineteenth Century Red and Green Appliqué Quilts," in *Kansas Quilts and Quilters*, Barbara Brackman et al. Lawrence, KS: University Press of Kansas, 1993.

_____, *Quilts in Red and Green: The Flowering of Folk Design in Nineteenth Century America*. Exhibit catalog. Wichita, KS: Wichita-Sedgwick County Historical Museum, 1992.

_____ and Terry Thompson, *Quilts in Red and Green and the Women Who Made Them*. Kansas City, MO: Kansas City Star Books, 2006.

Kimball, Jeana. *Red and Green: An Appliqué Tradition*. Bothell, WA: That Patchwork Place, 1990.

Nordstrom, Connie J., "Pot of Flowers Quilt Design," in *Uncoverings 2002, Vol.23. Lincoln, NE: Research Papers of the American Quilt Study Group*, 2002.

Ramsey, Bets, "Roses Real and Imaginary: Nineteenth Century Botanical Quilts of the Mid-South" in *Uncoverings 1986*. Vol 7, Mill Valley, CA, American Quilt Study Group, 1987.

Thompson, Terry Clothier, *Four Block Quilts: Echoes of History, Pieced Boldly & Appliquéd Freely*. Kansas City, MO: Kansas City Star Books, 2004.

_____, *The People of the Plains: Quilts and Stories*. Lenexa, KS: Peace Creek Pattern Company, 2002.

_____, Website, www:terrythompson.com

About the Authors

Nancy Hornback

Nancy Hornback grew up on the desert of southern California, where quiltmaking was not a part of the warm-weather environment. However, when she was a child, she would sometimes visit the grandmother of a neighbor family that had moved to California from the Ozarks. While sitting in a rocking chair, she would ask the elderly woman questions about her life. At the same time she could peer past her into a room that always had a beautiful quilt on a bed. When Nancy moved to Kansas, she had never actually seen a quilt being made until she started one of her own in 1973, learning from library books.

Now, Nancy researches quilts and quiltmakers, writes, lectures, curates exhibits, collects quilts and makes quilts. Besides her obvious enthusiasm for 19th Century floral quilts, she also finds great appeal in figurative appliqué and pictorial quilts, especially quilts with people figures on them. Her long-time interest in women's history and folk art motivates her research. She was a founding member of the Prairie Quilt Guild of Wichita, co-founder and board member of the Kansas Quilt Project, and served on the board of the American Quilt Study Group, She meets monthly with Quilt Lite, a small stitch group. She lives in Wichita, Kansas with her husband, Terry. They raised seven children and now have twenty grandchildren and one great-grandchild.

Terry Clothier Thompson

Terry Clothier Thompson has been on the forefront of our current quilt revival.

Born into the fifth generation of a Kansas pioneer family, she grew up in the Wichita area. She watched her grandmother sew and quilt during visits to this family farm called Peace Creek, west of Hutchinson, Kansas.

Her stitching passion began when she sewed calico dresses for her daughter. With the leftover scraps, she made a quilt. She became passionate.

Her family's move to Kansas City brought the opportunity to teach patchwork at Johnson County Community College. In 1973, she opened "The Quilting Bee," a store devoted totally to quilting, an anomaly at that time. The shop was located on the Country Club Plaza until 1984. She designed a unique line of patterns that she still sells nationwide. Terry was a principal documenter for the Kansas Quilt Project from 1986 to 1989 and was a co-author of *Kansas Quilts and Quilters*, published in 1993 by the University Press of Kansas.

In addition to her appliqué patterns, Terry has written six books, each a collection of family stories in different eras, with quilts designed to go along with the stories.

Her passion for quiltmaking is contagious. She has an extensive collection of vintage fabrics, quilts, laces, and all kinds of needlework. Terry's FabriCamp© classes are held in her new studio in Lawrence, Kansas. She also designs a line of reproduction fabrics for Moda. For more information about Terry, check out her web site: terrythompson.com.

She raised two children and enjoys her four wonderful grandchildren.